Business Models and Strategic Management

Business Models and Strategic Management

A New Integration

Francine Newth

business**expert**
Press

Business Models and Strategic Management: A New Integration
Copyright © Business Expert Press, 2012.

First published in 2012 by
Business Expert Press, LLC
222 East 46th Street, New York, NY 10017
www.businessexpertpress.com

ISBN-13: 978-1-60649-401-1 (paperback)

ISBN-13: 978-1-60649-402-8 (e-book)

DOI 10.4128/9781606494028

Business Expert Press Strategic Management collection

Collection ISSN: 2150-9611 (print)
Collection ISSN: 2150-9646 (electronic)

Cover design by Jonathan Pennell
Interior design by Exeter Premedia Services Private Ltd.,
Chennai, India

First edition: 2012

10 9 8 7 6 5 4 3 2 1

Printed in the United States of America.

To my two wonderful sons, Sean and Terrence, my source of inspiration.
To my late husband, Dennis, for loving me à l'infini.

Abstract

Do you manage to your business model? The purpose of this book is to provide the reader with the insights to strategically manage from a business model perspective. What does that mean? It means that managers have to first think rigorously about their value proposition, their current or future competencies, and their revenue streams and cost structure before developing, adopting, or modifying their strategies. What is the difference between a business model and a strategy? A business model is how a company operates and a strategy is how a company competes. When the basis of competition changes because a new model disrupts the economics in the industry (e.g., publishing and book retailing) it requires an adjustment in business models before any new strategy can work. This book adds a business model level to the traditional strategic management process to be more consistent with current "real-world" practices in strategic thinking and analysis. It takes the reader deeper into the intricacies of what constitutes a business model and how current strategy is derived from it. It is based on the premise that effective strategies cannot be formulated without understanding the fundamental elements of a business model.

This book offers seven modules. Module 1 identifies the key components of a business model to help conduct business model analysis. Module 2 presents a financial approach to assessing the financial viability of a business model while Module 3 provides the elements of setting a strategic direction to begin the implementation of a business model. Module 4 helps further understand how a company can operate with a business model given its capabilities and competencies to develop a sustainable competitive advantage. Module 5 looks at strategy from a dynamic capabilities perspective along with Module 6 on how innovation is integral to business model thinking and successful strategy implementation. Finally, Module 7 culminates into the business model agenda integrating the key concepts from the six modules to develop a business model-centric organization.

Keywords

business models, capabilities and competencies, competitive advantage, revenue streams, strategic direction, strategy, value creation for the business model-centric organization, value proposition, business model innovation, business model agenda

Contents

List of Figures

Acknowledgments

I am grateful to David Parker, the Publisher, and William Judge, the Collection Editor, for approving my proposal and believing in the value of this book. Without their support, this book would never have been written.

I am extremely appreciative of the work of Ngoc Pham, my bright and resourceful research assistant, who spent hours reading articles and helping to prepare materials for this book. I also express my appreciation to all my past and present students for their participation in class and for their motivation to learn more about business models.

I am very thankful for the support and insight of my sister, Ghislaine Larouche, who shared her knowledge of what it means to integrate concepts in the form of a new communication approach to learning.

I am particularly grateful to my sister-in-law, JoAnn Newth Sell, for her editorial review and her creative insights during this process as well as Rick Kreider for his meaningful edits.

Last but not least, I express my deep appreciation to John Migliaccio for always motivating me to be my best.

Introduction

I wrote this book to offer a new approach to strategic thinking that is simple and powerful. With years of teaching strategy and working on research projects with a variety of industries, I find that the new center of gravity in the field of strategic management is the business model. It is a phenomenon that needs to be explained to students and managers from the holistic perspective of how companies do business. It is full of opportunities for students and managers to be analytical and creative, and make a difference in the actions and decisions of businesses because they understand their company's business model. As a result, I wrote a unique book that lends itself to an interactive pedagogy rooted in student involvement as they will be required to be engaged learners and doers over the span of their careers. As this book teaches students and managers to understand the real drivers of successful outcomes, my key drivers for writing the book were to utilize my insights and experience to create easily navigable and instructional pathways. The readers can follow, explore, and understand the value-creating possibilities of a well-crafted business model.

The module approach breaks down the breadth of information provided in traditional strategy textbooks into *manageable learning projects*. Each module brings you on a journey to discover your creative mind by providing an insightful path with geometric shapes, boardroom pictures, and guidance points.

Geometric shapes are used throughout the modules because they act as mental keys to unlock your subconscious perceptions. Also you are asked to imagine each shape in color because colors favor actions.

What Is a Business Model?

Everything in the universe has shapes and colors. In each module, we use various geometric forms to help you find amazing connections and give rise to new ideas and insights.

"Seeing with our eyes, seeing with our minds."[1]

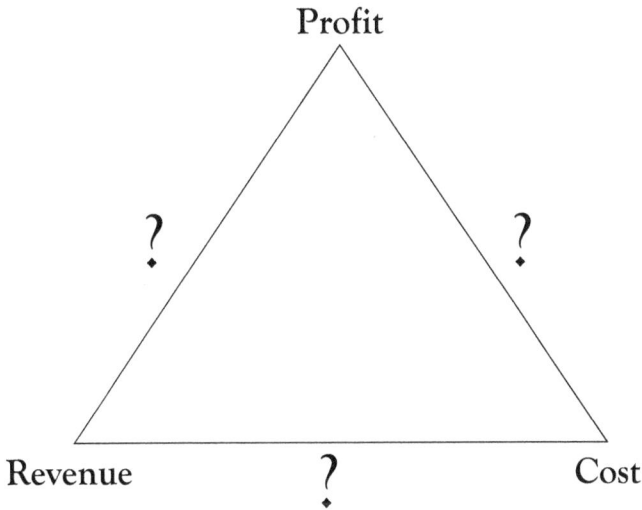

Profit

?   ?

Revenue   ?   Cost

In your view, how do the three elements of a business model interrelate? Use the triangle to write the key components that represent your concept of a business model before proceeding to the next page.

Imagine a green triangle to transform a business model

Objectives

1. Understand the concept of a business model.
2. Use real-world examples of business models interactively.
3. Develop a business model mind-set creatively.

Prelude

Albert Einstein said that imagination is more important than knowledge. So let's imagine for a moment …. Imagine knowing exactly what it takes for your organization to be innovative and profitable. As an employee, you know how to think about adding value in a sustainable way. You have the ability to clarify the value proposition of your business model that provides a clear focus for your organization. Your company's business model leads to exponential growth because it is aligned with the dynamics of your industry and the dynamics of your organization. You understand the business model and how you contribute to it in the processes that are in place. You know the capabilities and competencies and how the company makes money. You realize, however, that as industry dynamics change, business models are impacted. As such, you think creatively about new revenue streams, ways to decrease costs, enhance organizational capabilities, and strengthen the value proposition. In effect, you have the capacity to participate in expanding, rethinking, or fundamentally reinventing your company's business model.

Few managers can state what a business model is and most often misinterpret the term to mean strategy. The difference between a business model and a strategy is that a business model is an "internal system that is made up of components, linkages between components, and dynamics"[2] whereas a strategy is an external competitive approach using the capabilities that you have developed in your business model. A business model identifies the problem to be solved (customer need) and describes how your business will profit from addressing that need. Strategy, in contrast, is about how you will differentiate your business to give it a competitive advantage. Your business model will allow you to operate efficiently as a business in order to compete effectively and make the right strategy moves. Understanding what a business model is can change strategic decisions, operational decisions, and investment decisions to support the profit-making agenda in a meaningful way. It is said that a business model creates the value and a strategy captures it. Scholars view the business model as a new unit of analysis that seeks to explain how value is created and emphasizes system-level approach.[3] This module introduces you to the key components of a business model. It is the basis for understanding the business model-centric approach to strategic management. This book explains how organizations can clearly describe their business model and use it as a strategic management tool.

Characteristics of a Sound Business Model

A sound business model offers unique value (*value proposition*), builds barriers to entry through a bundle of resources (*dynamic capabilities and competencies*), and aligns the internal cost structure to the external revenue streams to achieve sustainable profits (*financial viability*). A business model is not simply a value proposition, or revenue stream, or capability, or a cost structure. What makes it a "model to do business" successfully is the proper combination of all these elements working together. "When business models don't work, it's because they fail either the narrative test (the story doesn't make sense) or the numbers test (the P&L doesn't add up)."[4] The components of a business model are shown in Figure 1.

The logic for using a triangle to describe a business model is that it has "the most hidden complexity in an apparently simple form."[5] Similarly, the worth of a simple idea turned into a business model is in the complexity

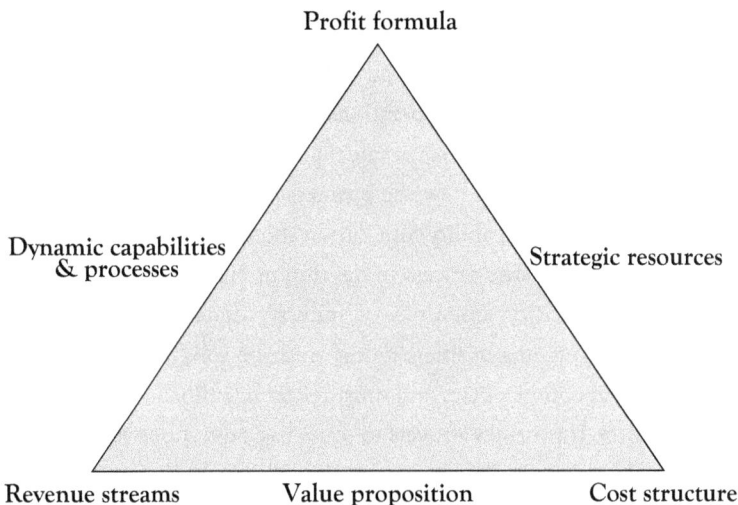

Profit formula

Dynamic capabilities & processes

Strategic resources

Revenue streams

Value proposition

Cost structure

Figure 1. Components of a business model.

of the operations commonly referred to as "hard to copy." The more unity among the components, the more value. The value proposition is at the base of the triangle because it is the starting point in the development of an idea. Moving along the sides of the triangle, to make the idea work, certain resources or key assets need to be attuned and strategically deployed in processes to build deep capabilities and competencies. The strategic resources are on the cost structure side because financial resources are required to acquire them. They also appear on the revenue side when they are properly used in a dynamic process to generate revenues. Think of Southwest Airlines and how they developed an idea to revolutionize the cost of flying in the United States. They built operations based on new dynamic processes by training their employees for quick turnaround of planes and flying those planes from one destination to another as opposed to a hub. As a result of these new employee and systems capabilities, they developed a business model that could challenge the "hub-and-spoke" model of all the existing airlines.

Moving to the corners of the triangles, the revenue streams can be projected, the cost structure of the operations can be priced, and the profit formula can be derived. Together all the business model components represent the basics of business model thinking for the manager. The triangle is also a cognitive tool to help you think comprehensively and rigorously about your business model.

What Is a Business Model?

A business model explains how you will monetize your idea and make money with your method of operations, based on your capabilities and competencies to carry out your value proposition. A business model involves the conception of how the business must operate given its value proposition, what its capability foundation should be, and whether it can be financially viable. The process to develop or change a business model revolves around critical questions of industry dynamics and company dynamics. A company's business model must be solidly grounded in its capabilities and competencies and must reflect or influence the dynamics of the industry. It provides answers to some basic questions such as "How will we make money?" "What capabilities will it take to have profitable operations?" "How will we generate sales and profits?" "How will we sustain revenue growth?" "How will we sustain income growth?"

A business model has three qualitative components: a value proposition, strategic resources, and dynamic processes. A value proposition is the development of an idea that fills a gap in customer experiences or creates an important customer want. For example, the value proposition of Pandora Media is to provide free access to online radio service.[6] For Twitter, it is to allow anyone to interact socially with virtually anyone else.[7] A strategic resource is a strategic asset used to develop capabilities in the company's value chain. A dynamic process is the right mix of strategic resources used in a company's operations that builds capability and competencies. For example, the competencies of Pandora Media are customer options and accurate musical preferences based on artist, title, or genre.[8] For Twitter it is ease of use, accessibility on a variety of devices, and instantaneous information availability.[9] Strategic resources and dynamic processes to develop competencies are discussed in Module 4, Business Model and Competitive Advantage.

Once the value proposition, strategic resources, and dynamic processes are in place, the ultimate test of a business model lies in its three quantitative components: revenue sources, cost structure, and profitability. These components make up the profit formula for your business model. Revenues should come from as many sources of revenues as possible, that is, subscriptions, transactions, licensing fees (see the Revenue Sources section). Cost-reduction opportunities should come from those costs that are not conducive to real value or from improving benefits at the same or lower costs. For example, a change in technology can result in cost reductions and an improved business model. Adding features to a product without raising prices or increasing costs improves a business model. Profitability comes from more sources of revenues, fewer costs, and more value. It is the test of financial viability which manifests itself in profit margins.

Revenue Sources

Revenue sources include the following bases of revenue streams:

- Product based
- Service based
- Subscription based
- Transaction based (fee per transaction)
- Rent based (pay per use)

- Royalty based (licensing)
- Advertising based.

Both Pandora Media and Twitter's revenue streams are advertising based.[10] Assessing revenues is no longer only a manufacturing, marketing, or distribution issue; it is a business-model issue that focuses on whether the business model can generate enough revenue. Management must continuously adapt their business model to capture different revenue streams. Another example is Yahoo! Yahoo!'s management has adapted their business model from strictly advertising-based revenues to include service-based revenues. Their business model was no longer effective due to advertisers significantly reducing their presence by lowering their media purchases or in some cases, simply going out of business.[11]

Cost Structure

The cost structure is guided by a company's value chain and competencies. A value chain is a tool to identify the operational areas where capabilities and competencies exist. In turn, these competencies contribute to profit margins. A sustainable business model requires investments for innovation and productivity in areas such as operations, marketing, technology, human resources, and logistics. These investments help strengthen competencies that are the foundation of the business model. Management must ask what organizational capabilities and competencies need to be developed or improved in order to support the revenue and income objectives. Investment into critical areas, based on the value chain, will determine a firm's profitability. Costs are incurred to develop capabilities. The business model costs of Pandora Media are paying royalties for music;[12] while for Twitter it is the technology platform and its maintenance.[13]

Profit Formula

People often think a profit formula is a business model, but how you make a profit is only one piece of the model. It consists of the revenue streams, cost structure (assets, costs, if and how economies of scale impact costs), profit margins (how much each transaction needs to net to cover the cost structure and deliver target profits), and resource velocity (how much revenue needs to be generated per dollar of assets and per dollar of fixed costs and how quickly). For more discussion of a profit formula see suggested readings at the end of Module 2.

Profitability

A company's ability to generate revenues with an appropriate cost structure results in profitability. Revenues are driven by the market demand for a company's products or services and from business operations embedded in the capabilities and competencies of a company's value chain. A company's business model can only be as sound as its competencies and its understanding of the industry. The result is profitability or loss. Profitability or loss is proof of the financial viability or nonviability of a business model. We often hear the management of franchised firms referring to the evidence that their business model works. They have proven business models because of their uniquely developed systems and processes, their profit model, and their value proposition. They have key operational metrics embedded in their management processes such as sales metrics, on-time delivery metrics, supplier performance metrics. These metrics are the ongoing performance measurements of the revenues and cost structure. They do lead to profitability if the company's market position and its value-chain competencies are aligned.

How Do You Develop or Rethink a Business Model?

There are three action steps to consider when you want to develop or rethink a business model.

Step 1: Consider the Dynamics in Your Industry and Related Industries

Finding trends or shifts will help assess whether or not industry dynamics are changing. Consider related industries as potentially new value propositions that are often born from a convergence of related fields. This will help clarify the real context in which you operate and will facilitate discovering how to rethink your business model or develop a new business model.

Discuss the future as you perceive it: Look for recent changes and challenges in your industry. Describe those changes and challenges and their impact on your business model. Imagine what your industry will look like in the future. Look at the change in demand for your products or services, and how the consumer-buying behaviors might be different. Consider if the competitors have changed and how the new competitors might be different. Recognize that there might be new capabilities and competencies to succeed in the industry and how you can develop or acquire them. Reflect on how the industry supply chain might have changed such as having suppliers with more scale affecting your cost structure or having competitors with more integrated operations. It may mean having more or less outsourcing and insourcing. Be aware of the fact that your industry might be more global as a result of mergers and acquisitions.

Take action: An example of a company that has assessed the dynamics in their industry is FedEx. As a result, FedEx is predicting an industry shift. Why? Some of the dynamics are changing. They include more competition from seaborne shipping as customers are increasingly choosing nonpremium delivery services. How did they know? The demand for their product was changing. Revenues for express shipping grew by 2.6% but operating profits declined by 35%, while ground shipping revenues grew by 9.7% with an 18% increase in operating margins. The traditional "airport-to-airport business" is not growing.[14]

The next step will reveal whether FedEx should adjust their operations.

Step 2: Assess Your Company Dynamics

This step focuses on understanding whether or not you have the capabilities and competencies to create new industry dynamics or respond to them.

Discuss your company: Identify the capabilities and competencies in your value chain. If needed, invest in new capabilities and competencies to create and capture more value for your customers, stockholders, management, and employees. Develop crossfunctional teams for meaningful integration and efficiencies. Have knowledge of the source metrics to allow for quick adjustments.

Take action: To continue with our FedEx example, Mr. Smith cites that FedEx has "scale and combined air, ground, and freight capabilities" putting it in a strong position to respond to the shifting trends. In particular, its freight-forward business, FedEx Trade Networks, has capabilities in logistical services and third-party shipping including via sea.[15] As much as there will always be demand for premium air delivery, a new focus for FedEx is on value-added customized delivery services which include, for example, tracking capabilities. So it appears that FedEx has the capabilities and competencies to respond to the shift in demand, while taking advantage of new opportunities to begin to create new dynamics in shipping.[16]

Step 3: Rethink the Business Model

This last step focuses on whether or not you need to rethink your business model and take action. This last step helps you to consider all the components of your business model and the relationships among those components. Think about what adding to or honing in on a capability can do to your operating performance. Rethinking your business model or tweaking it can be done by evaluating your value proposition, cutting costs, adding to capabilities, and seeking new revenue streams.

Discuss your business model: Think about your value proposition and whether it is still relevant vis-à-vis your customers, your capabilities and competencies, and your existing and emerging competitors. Adjust and streamline your cost structure to your revenue streams and keep seeking new revenue streams to accommodate your cost structure. Examine how your profit formula can be more profitable.

Take action: Within the context of the FedEx business model and their industry changes and challenges, FedEx decided to seek new revenue streams by offering more value-added services with existing capabilities. They will also cut costs under the guidance of a "comprehensive plan." Additionally they will align their express fleet capabilities to new market demand.[17]

Business Model Applications

To interactively learn the process of developing or rethinking a business model, below are

1. Three interactive "Enter the Boardroom" applications to learn how to use the key components of a business model at the strategic level of the organization.
2. One exercise to develop your business model analytical skills.

1. Enter the Boardroom Interactive Applications

The "Enter the Boardroom" series consist of brief stories of companies to illustrate key concepts in each module. Imagine that you are an independent board member questioning decisions made by applying the concepts you learned. To be in an interactive learning environment, read each company scenario below with the corresponding concept and reflect on who should be at the table, what the agenda should consist of, and what the outcome(s) might be. This will also give you some thoughts for your own questions.

Enter the Boardroom Series: The Business Model

Netflix, Wal-Mart, eBay

What Is a Value Proposition? The Netflix Story

A value proposition is usually a product or a service or a way to operate which costs less and delivers *more value at the same price, less value at a lower price, or much more value at a greater price.* Sometimes it is simply a new idea with which a company can generate new revenues because the idea delivers value with the company's competencies and dynamic capabilities. Once you decide how a business can bring superior value to a market segment, you can begin to determine whether or not it will be financially viable. A value proposition responds to an important customer need that usually comes from an insight into what is not being offered or a gap in service or product. For example, the original value proposition for Netflix was to provide movie rentals without charging late fees. The insight came from challenging the assumption by asking "What if we did something that nobody else is doing; what if we could rent a movie and not have to charge a late fee for those who return the movies late?" Wow … wouldn't that be a great value proposition! Netflix built an organization to carry out this value proposition. Others copied and new technology was developed which created new

(*Continued*)

challenges for Netflix.[18] (For more information on the Netflix model, read the article cited in the notes and references starting on p. 157.)

Enter the Netflix Boardroom

Who should be in the boardroom?
What is the agenda?
Why?

You are now a board member of Netflix Inc. Be prepared to answer the following questions:

1. What were the changes in industry dynamics?
2. Why did Netflix have to rethink its value proposition?
3. How is Netflix meeting or not meeting customer expectations?

Prepare your own questions for the other members of the board:

4. What …
5. Why …
6. How …
7. Other questions.

(Continued)

What Is a Dynamic Capability? The Wal-Mart Story

It is a new configuration of the way an organization uses its resources. It is a firm's ability to integrate, build, and reconfigure internal and external resources to address rapidly changing environments. You can build dynamic capabilities in your business processes by changing the way you operate. Wal-Mart's value proposition is to sell national brands at everyday low prices. To deliver on this value, Wal-Mart needed to develop dynamic capabilities in purchasing, logistics, and management information systems. They developed innovative ways to improve the efficient use of their resources to reduce costs, deliver value, and achieve superior performance.[19] (For more information on Wal-Mart, read the article cited in the notes and references starting on p. 157.)

Enter the Wal-Mart Boardroom

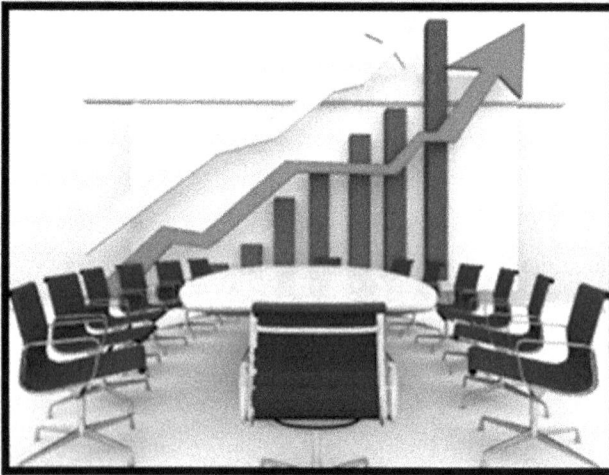

Who should be in the boardroom?
What is the agenda?
Why?

(Continued)

You are now a board member of Wal-Mart. Be prepared to answer the following questions:

1. What did Wal-Mart choose to do differently?
2. Why was Wal-Mart able to offer a different kind of value?
3. How did Wal-Mart develop dynamic capabilities?

Prepare your own questions for the other members of the board:

1. What ...
2. Why ...
3. How ...
4. Other questions.

What Is Financial Viability? The eBay Story

Your value proposition will deliver profits when the scope of your activities results in an appropriate cost structure. When *eBay* was first conceptualized, the founders realized that the business idea could only achieve the scale effect online. They also decided that the scope of their business would never include, for example, carrying an inventory or paying for transportation. As a result, the financial viability of this online auction business model pointed to huge revenue streams with minimal costs.[20] (For more information on eBay, read the article cited in the notes and references starting on p. 157.)

(Continued)

Enter the eBay Boardroom

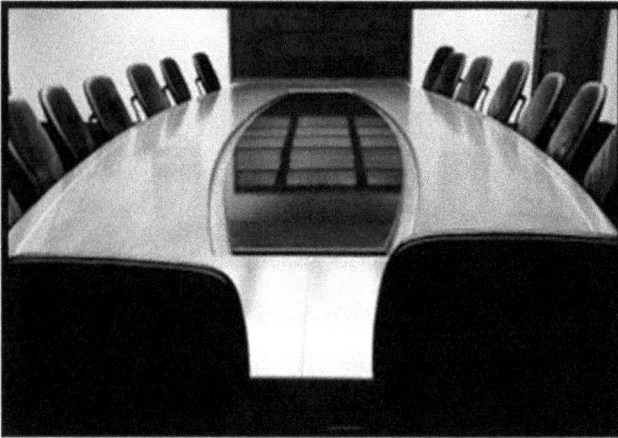

Who should be in the boardroom?
What is the agenda?
Why?

You are now a board member of eBay. Be prepared to answer the following questions:

1. What assumptions did eBay make on the profitability of their business model?
2. Why did eBay become so successful?
3. How did eBay sustain their revenue and income growth?

Prepare your own questions for the other members of the board:

4. What …
5. Why …
6. How …
7. Other questions.

2. Business Model Matrix Analysis

One way to analyze a business model is to run two critical tests: a narrative test and a numbers test.[21] For the purpose of the exercise, both the narrative test (whether the story makes sense) and the numbers test are adapted to provide a more focused value test (V test) and quantitative test (Q test). The V test includes the three qualitative components of a business model: value proposition, strategic resources, and dynamic processes. The Q test includes the three quantitative components of a business model's financial viability: the growth in revenues, the underlying cost structure of operating margins, and profitability. The findings of the two tests are viewed side-by-side in a business model matrix which identifies the relationships between the "story" and the "numbers" and points to their potential impact on your business model.

Business Model Matrix Exercise

1. Select an industry and two companies within that industry. (Use of value line or Moody's is recommended for this exercise.)
2. Conduct the following two tests:
   a. The Q test (quantitative): provide 3 years of trend data in sales growth %, operating margin %, net profit margin % for each company and for the industry (use industry % as base % to draw conclusions).
   b. The V test (value): describe each company's value proposition, strategic resources, dynamic capabilities, as well as current industry dynamics.
3. Develop a business model matrix (see sample on the next page).
4. Draw conclusions between the findings of the Q test and the V test.
5. Make recommendations as an analyst.

Sample Business Model Matrix

	Q Test			V Test		
	Revenue growth (3-yr line)	Operating margins (3-yr line)	Net margins (3-yr line)	Value proposition (VP)	Strategic resources (SR)	Dynamic capabilities/ competencies
Industry				(For industry use rate of change) Circle one: H M L	N/A	N/A
Company A				VP:	SR:	DC:
Company B				VP:	SR:	DC:
Business Model Impact (BMI) Circle one: High (H) Medium (M) Low (L)	For example: New revenue streams needed: H M L	For example: Cost structure efficiencies needed: H M L	For example: Better returns needed: H M L	For example: Evidence of adequate demand and acceptable returns for VP needed: H M L	For example: Strategic resources needed: H M L	For example: New capabilities needed: H M L

Note: The first three columns help you track your profit formula. However, financial performance trends are laggard indicators. They do not drive performance. They are the results of operating efficiencies and metrics (Module 2). In this exercise, you develop your analytical skills of the qualitative and quantitative nature of your operations and the impact on your business model .

Guidance for the Manager:

Key Points on Business Models

- Your business model is only as good as your understanding of its components.
- Closely look at your operations to recognize your strategic resources and your dynamic processes.
- Use a 3 step process to rethink your business model.
- A business model starts with a value proposition which is supported by how the business operates with its strategic resources and dynamic capabilities.
- It reflects the competency foundation of the whole enterprise.
- It is an entire system of delivering value to customers and making a profit.
- A business model answers some basic questions such as How can we make money? Can we have profitable operations? How can we generate sales and income? How can we sustain revenue growth and income growth? Can we achieve financial viability?
- The profit formula includes:

    1. Revenue Sources as bases of revenue streams. Examples include product-based, service-based, subscription-based, transaction-based (fee per transaction), rent-based (pay per use), and royalty-based.
    Revenues should come from as many sources as possible as a result of product expansions and segmentation of your products and markets. Value chain competencies will impact prices and ability to price competitively.
    2. Cost Structure
    The costs of organizational capabilities needed to support your revenue and income objectives.
    Your investments into critical competency areas must be based on your value chain which will determine your profitability.

(Continued)

3. Profitability

The profitability of your business model is in the fit between your sources of revenue and your cost structure. The test of financial viability is in your profit margins. If it's profitable, your business model works.

Add your own key points:

Now that you have applied the concept of a business model in different applications, let's look at the relationship between a business model and the various components of strategically managing an organization. Below is a brief overview of the remaining modules. The end result is Module 7 that integrates the first six modules into a business model agenda.

- *Business Model and Financial Management*
  Module 2 presents a financial approach to assessing the financial viability of a business model with a specific focus on the drivers of revenue streams, cost of activities, and financial management decisions.
- *Business Model and Strategic Direction*
  Module 3 focuses on the core elements of setting a strategic direction. Once you have a promising business model you need to articulate your vision, mission, strategies, and performance objectives. The business model is the internal engine where the pieces of a business fit together. The strategic direction provides the fuel to keep it running and the lubrication for needed adjustments.
- *Business Model and Competitive Advantage*
  Module 4 brings your attention to the use of resources to develop dynamic capabilities and competencies to achieve a competitive advantage. If you use your resources in different ways, like Southwest Airlines' quick turnaround of planes allowing them to charge less and still maintain their level of profitability due to more frequent flights, you can build dynamic capabilities to give your company a competitive advantage.
- *Business Model and Strategy*
  Module 5 looks at strategy from a dynamic capability perspective and explains how strategies support the business model. Strategies are the choices you make regarding whether or not you have the business model to execute on a market opportunity.
- *Business Model and Innovation*
  Module 6 looks at how innovation and change in an organization are integral to business model thinking. The capacity

to innovate in an organization is essential to make a business model sustainable.

- *Business Model Agenda*

  Module 7 culminates in a collaborative agenda as a framework to assess the components of a business model-centric organization. The priorities of the business model agenda fit into the strategic plan, the financial plan, and the operational plan.

Below is a recommended Harvard Business Publishing case available for purchase at: www.hbsp.harvard.edu

Zipcar: Refining the Business Model

Myra M. Hart; Michael J. Roberts; Julia D. Stevens
Product Number: 803096-PDF-ENG
Publication Date: May 09, 2005
Length: 20 pages

Description:

"Zipcar is a start-up organized around the idea of 'sharing' car usage via a membership organization. This case describes several iterations of the Zipcar business model and financial plan. These iterations include a very early version and a version developed just prior to the launch of the business, as well as data from the first few months of operations. Students are called on to analyze the underlying economics and business model for the venture and to discover how these assumptions are holding up as the business is actually rolled out."

Link to Module 1: This case focuses on continuously looking at the business model and its metrics.

Below are recommended Harvard Business School Publishing articles available for purchase at: www.hbsp.harvard.edu

Why Business Models Matter

Joan Magretta
Product Number: R0205F-PDF-ENG
Publication date: May 01, 2002
Length: 6 pages

Description:

"Business model" was one of the great buzzwords of the Internet boom. A company didn't need a strategy, a special competence, or even any customers—all it needed was a web-based business model that promised wild profits in some distant, ill-defined future. Many people—investors, entrepreneurs, and executives alike—fell for the fantasy and got burned. And as the inevitable counter reaction played out, the concept of the business model fell out of fashion nearly as quickly as the .com appendage itself. That's a shame. As Joan Magretta explains, a good business model remains essential to every successful organization, whether it's a new venture or an established player. To help managers apply the concept successfully, she defines what a business model is and how it complements a smart competitive strategy. Business models are, at heart, stories that explain how enterprises work. Like a good story, a robust business model contains precisely delineated characters, plausible motivations, and a plot that turns on an insight about value. It answers certain questions: Who is the customer? How do we make money? What underlying economic logic explains how we can deliver value to customers at an appropriate cost? Every viable organization is built on a sound business model, but a business model isn't a strategy, even though many people use the terms interchangeably. Business models describe, as a system, how the pieces of a business fit together. But they don't factor in one critical dimension of performance: competition. That's the job of strategy. Illustrated with examples from companies such as American Express, Euro Disney, Wal-Mart, and Dell Computer, this article explains the difference between business models and strategy, which are fundamental to every company's performance."

Link to Module 1: This article provides clear examples of the difference between a business model and a strategy.

Reinventing Your Business Model

M. W. Johnson; C. M. Christensen; H. Kagermann
Product Number: R0812C-PDF-ENG
Publication date: December 01, 2008
Length: 12 pages

Description:

"This article includes a one-page preview that quickly summarizes the key ideas and provides an overview of how the concepts work in practice along with suggestions for further reading. Why is it so difficult for established companies to pull off the new growth that business model innovation can bring? Here's why: They don't understand their current business model well enough to know if it would suit a new opportunity or hinder it, and they don't know how to build a new model when they need it. Drawing on their vast knowledge of disruptive innovation and experience in helping established companies capture game-changing opportunities, consultant Johnson, Harvard Business School professor Christensen, and SAP co-CEO Kagermann set out the tools that executives need to do both. Successful companies already operate according to a business model that can be broken down into four elements: a customer value proposition that fulfills an important job for the customer in a better way than anything competitors offer; a profit formula that lays out how the company makes money delivering the value proposition; and the key resources and key processes needed to deliver that proposition. Game-changing opportunities deliver radically new customer-value propositions: They fulfill a job to be done in a dramatically better way (as P&G did with its Swiffer mops), solve a problem that's never been solved before (as Apple did with its iPod and iTunes electronic entertainment delivery system), or serve an entirely unaddressed customer base (as Tata Motors is doing with its Nano—the $2,500 car aimed at Indian families who can't afford any other type of car and usually use motorcycles to get around). Doing so doesn't always require a new business model, but a new model is called for under certain conditions. It is often needed to leverage a new technology (as in Apple's case); is generally required when the opportunity addresses an entirely new group of customers (as with the Nano); and is surely in order when an established company needs to fend off a successful disruptor (as the Nano's competitors will now need to do)."

Link to Module 1: This article provides in-depth discussion about value proposition, key resources and processes, and profit formula.

The Great Repeatable Business Model

Chris Zook; James Allen

Product number: R1111G-PDF-ENG

Publication date: November 01, 2011

Length: 9 pages

Description:

"The sharper a company's differentiation, the greater its competitive advantage. In studying companies that sustained a high level of performance over many years, the authors, both partners at Bain, have found that more than 80% of them had a well-defined and easily understood differentiation at the center of strategy. But differentiation can wear with age: The growth it generates creates complexity, and complex companies tend to forget what they're good at. Often they respond by trying to reimagine their entire business models quickly and dramatically. That's rarely the answer, the authors write. Really successful companies relentlessly build on their fundamental differentiation, going from strength to strength. They learn to deliver it to the front line, creating an organization that lives and breathes its strategic advantages day in and day out. They learn to sustain it through constant adaptation to changes in the market. And they learn to resist the siren song of today's hot market better than their less-focused competitors do. The result is a simple, repeatable business model that a company can apply to new products and markets over and over again to generate sustained growth."

Link to Module 1: This article explains the sustainability of a business model.

Note: Descriptions are from www.hbsp.harvard.edu with permission.

Reflect on what you originally included on the first page of this module and how your understanding of a business model has changed. Are you ready to rethink your business model and take action? (See Appendix A for samples of successful business models.)

MODULE 2

Business Model and Financial Management

Building on the triangle from Module 1, in this module we use the geometric form of a square which consists of four triangles to demonstrate the interrelationships of the components of the business model to financial management.

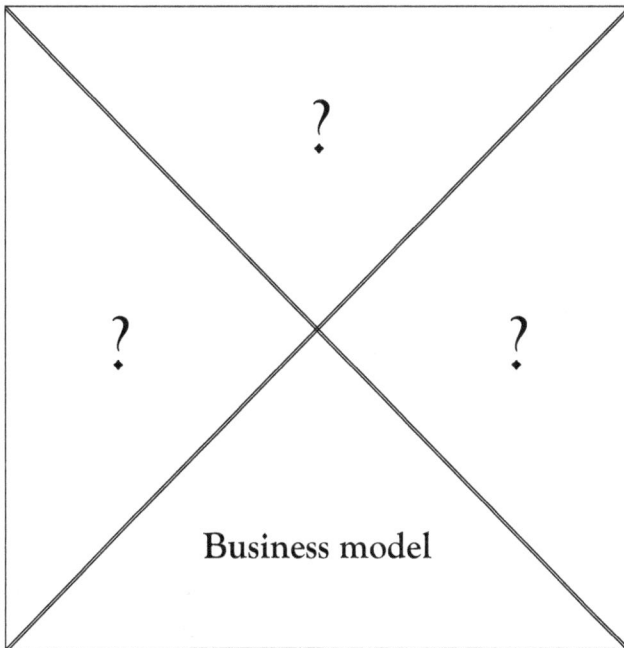

In your view, what is the relationship between a business model and financial management? Use the three triangles to write the key components that represent your concept of critical areas of financial performance that are integral to a business model before going to the next page.

Imagine a blue square to expand your perspective on financial management

Objectives

1. Understand the relationship between business model and financial management.
2. Use real-world examples of financial results.
3. Discuss financial management decisions.

Prelude

"A recurring theme is that a business must be viewed as an integrated whole and that effective financial management is possible only within the context of a company's broader operating characteristics and strategies."[1] In this module, financial management is defined as an integrated approach, a business model view of how to look at the financial performance of a company. It consists of bringing together three aspects of financial management: strategic planning, financial analysis, and financial decisions, to better manage the performance of a business model.

Strategic planning includes three subplans: the strategic plan, the operational plan, and the financial plan. Together these three plans support the business model of a company. As such, the strategic plan includes the value proposition, the objectives, and the strategies for a three-to-five-year period; the operational plan addresses the strategic resources, the capabilities, and the dynamic processes needed to achieve the objectives and successfully implement the strategies; the financial plan lays out the financing requirements and return on investment (ROI) expectations to implement the strategic and operational plans. Financial analysis is narrowly focused on the metrics behind the numbers as it is a more useful analysis to understand the financial performance of a business model. It presents a financial approach to assessing the viability of a business model with a specific focus on the drivers of revenues, costs, and profits. Financial decisions are made to achieve the objectives stated in the strategic plan, the operational plan, and the financial plan to support the business model. There are three areas of financial decisions: decisions that are made to invest in operations (key capabilities of the business model), decisions made to finance the investment decisions, and decisions made on what to do with the money (profits), reinvest, distribute or both.

The contribution of this module is to focus on the financial implications of the business model in terms of growing the revenues of a company, restructure its costs, improve its profitability, enhance its cash flows, and invest in capabilities to create more value from its business model. The financial viability of a business model shows how a company can operate profitably given its revenue streams and costs of processes and capabilities.

Characteristics of Sound Financial Management

The antecedents or preconditions of sound financial management include knowing the underlying assumptions of the strategic plan and the metrics that drive the operational plan. Together these two factors provide insight into company performance in order to both develop the financial plan and analyze financial results.

Assumptions

All financial projections are based on strategic assumptions about your capabilities, your customers, and your markets. Google's revenue machine has slowed down not because consumers are clicking on their ads less frequently—in fact that metric rose by 34% in the last quarter of 2011—but because the average amount paid by advertisers fell by 8%. Why? And how is this impacting the existing assumption that more clicks equal more revenues? The answer is that ads on mobile devices cost less than ads on desktops. As more people access the web with their mobile devices, Google's ad revenues are negatively affected. Therefore, a new assumption to be tested could be: "Do more graphical and interactive ads equal more revenues?"[2]

From a business model point of view the impact of developing new market-based assumptions as a result of insight into customer use of products and services and the competitive space leads to new strategic choices, new revenues, and expanded markets. Again, let's take a look at Google's moves. Google acquired YouTube in 2006 and spent an additional $4 billion to acquire several other display ad technology companies for the needed capabilities. They are now selling graphical and video display ads which now account for Google's second biggest revenue stream generating $5 billion per year or over 10% of its overall revenue! The competitive space includes Facebook, the leader, followed by Yahoo!, Google, Microsoft, and AOL.[3]

Metrics

Metrics are measures of business performance. There are two types of metrics: operational metrics and financial metrics. Operational metrics are the *key drivers* and they really drive your company performance [e.g., customers per car (Zipcar), profit per dress (Rent the Runway)]. Financial metrics are key results [e.g., return on assets (ROA), sales, profits]. Operational metrics drive financial metrics. In the case of Google, the metric for ad revenue is "paid clicks." As the metric fluctuates up or down, the impact on revenue can be predicted and actions can be taken. Setting the appropriate metrics and tracking them is a key capability essential to support your business model.

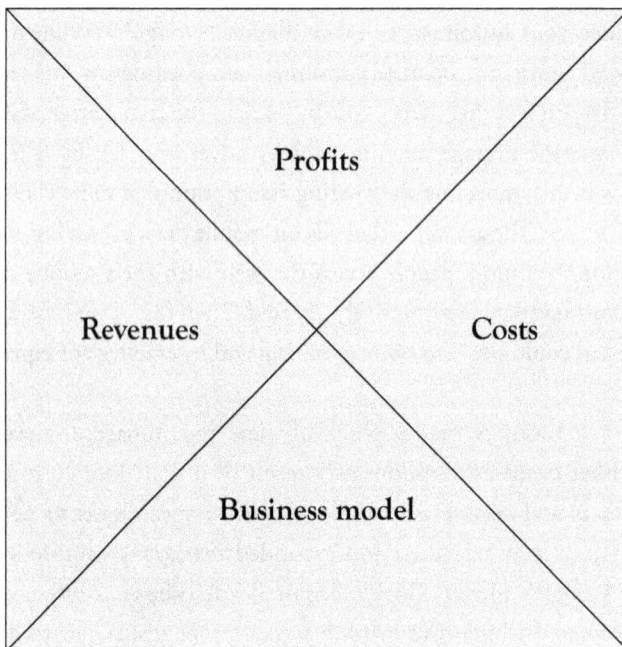

Figure 2. Financial components of a business model.

One of the best ways to use metrics is to wrap them around your business model. In other words, it is to make sure that the metrics are aligned with your key resources, capabilities, and dynamic processes that constitute the source of delivering the value proposition. This way the metrics can point to needed adjustments in the business model and behave as drivers of revenues, drivers of costs, and drivers of profits.

Financial Analysis

The drivers of costs in a business model are the resources and the processes used in a company's operations. They are part of how your business model creates value using a value chain to determine operating efficiencies. Your cost structure, also called a *cost model,* therefore helps to optimize your profit formula and stimulate future performance. In accounting and finance terms, cost structures are operating budgets using a ratio of fixed costs to variable costs to produce the highest profitability. In business model terms, costs structures represent cost drivers that add value.

When revenues grow and profits decrease, operating expenses are increasing. There is a lack of operating leverage. The impact of increasing operating costs on the top and bottom lines often raises business model questions. When the added spending and costs are to strengthen, enhance or protect the value proposition, the higher costs are easily justified and often fall in the realm of investments. Let's examine Amazon's formula for quick sales growth. First, let's consider the industry assumption that Internet sales is growing at a rate of 10% per year. Compare that to Amazon's revenue growth which has been more than 40% at times. However, operating expenses have risen by 38% for the fourth quarter of 2011; this resulted in operating margins of 1.5% compared to 3.8% in 2010. The cost increases have been much greater than the revenue growth but the business model calls for new products such as the Kindle Fire and building a bigger revenue generating platform with their "Prime Program" subscribers and their third-party retailers on its marketplace.

The relationship between your business model and the financial performance of your company starts with understanding what drives the costs of activities that a firm performs to build its resources into dynamic processes and fitting the cost structure to the revenue streams in order to achieve acceptable profit margins. The test of a company's financial viability is based on its profit margins as a result of operational and financial metrics. Operational metrics are cost drivers, revenue drivers, and profit drivers (the term driver is used as a metric). Together they contribute to financial metrics, the laggard indicators of financial performance, such as ROA, ROI, and return on equity, as well as gross, operating and net profit margins.

Cost Driver Analysis

The cost of doing business is critical to the success of a business model. One way to analyze costs as part of a business model is to conduct a cost analysis that focuses on cost drivers. It begins with assigning costs and assets to your value chain and determining the elements that drive the costs of each value activity. Once done, consider reconfiguring your value chain to control or decrease costs. Finally, conduct experiments by testing your operations to ensure that the cost savings are sustainable and strengthen your business model with hard-to-copy activities. Examples of cost drivers for Zipcar are cost per new member and member retention cost.

Revenue Driver Analysis

The revenue streams are equally critical to the success of a business model. One way to analyze revenues as part of a business model is to conduct a revenue analysis focused on revenue drivers. The drivers of revenue are either rooted in the buyer's purchase criteria or in units of revenue (e.g., usage revenue per car per day or revenue per member—Zipcar). You can determine the buyers' purchase criteria by analyzing the value your products or services offer to them. If it is a low-cost product or service or a differentiated product or service, why are they buying it? Besides looking at buyer motivation to determine revenue drivers, examine new revenue models to better reach the purchase criteria and perhaps even create a new revenue stream. For example, Netflix's service to download movies appeals to buyers' convenience criteria and on-demand flexibility criteria as it offers more value (more convenience, more flexibility) than the original mail-in revenue model. The revenue driver to track for convenience might be the number of downloads daily. Any fluctuations might provide insight into a new revenue stream.

Profit Driver Analysis

Profitability is ultimately the real indicator of the success of a business model. Profits tell you if your model is working. One way to analyze profits as part of a business model is to conduct a profit analysis focused on profit drivers. There are three major profit drivers: price, costs, and revenues (volume). To have a realistic view of profitability, you need to have a business model understanding of these profit driver areas. We have previously discussed the drivers of costs and revenues. Therefore, price as a profit driver will be the focus. Price is first determined by measuring costs. Having an internal activity-based accounting system to determine the size and sources of costs (fixed and variable) can help drive profits higher provided the value chain has an optimal configuration based on a company's capabilities and dynamic processes. In addition, a company's ability to build value into its products and services allows for more flexibility in pricing.

Financial Management Decisions

So far we have focused on the drivers of revenue streams, cost structure, and profitability to understand financial analysis from a business model perspective. The traditional view of financial analysis is to use financial data to evaluate the performance, condition, or future prospects of an organization. There are two primary sources of company financial data: the annual report and 10-K report. The management discussion in the 10-K report is particularly useful because management discusses the scope of their operations, what has worked well and what has not worked, future strategies, the competition, and any needed changes to improve performance. Financial analysis also includes the analysis of ratios among the financial statements. The income statement is a summary of revenues and expenses during a defined period (the "accounting period"); the balance sheet is a list of what a company owes and what it owns at one point in time; the cash flow statement shows a company's uses and sources of cash as well as the changes in a company's cash position during an accounting period. The financial statements inform financial management decisions. There are three decisions in financial management for growing the business model: the investment decision (capital budgeting), the financing decision (capital structure), and the dividend and stock buyback decision (use of capital).

The Investment Decision

Once a company decides it needs to grow to sustain or improve its revenues and profits, it must make some decisions to invest. Although cutting costs is one way to improve the bottom line, real sustainable growth requires specific investments that leverage core capabilities. Companies can minimize risk by investing in areas guided by their business model, their competencies, and their strategic and financial objectives. There are two basic choices: internal project investment and external acquisitions investment. As mentioned in the Prelude of this module, this is where the strategic plan, the operational plan, and the financial plan come together. The process starts at the strategic level with the strategic plan articulating the strategic goals for the next three to five years. The operating managers then develop the operational plan which translates the strategic goals into action plans with specific investment proposals. *Pro forma* financial statements are developed to demonstrate the financial implications of the operational plan with a particular focus on the cash flows. Lastly, the *capital budgeting* process which is the financial evaluation of investment proposals leads to the investment decision(s) and eventually the financial plan.

Internal project investment: A project which meets the internal rate of return as stated in the strategic plan using average rate of return, payback period, and discounted cash flows.

External acquisition investment: A proposed acquisition which can be valued by net worth (what a firm owns: stockholders' equity), future value (5 × average cash flows over the last five years), or P/E ratio for publicly traded firms [what a firm earns: stock price/earnings per share (EPS) × average profit (last five years)].

The Financing Decision

Now that you know where to invest, you need to finance those investments. Again you have two basic choices: internal financing and external financing. The sources of internal financing are primarily your retained earnings. The sources of external financing are debt and equity or creditors and investors. Both have risks and returns which leads us to the concept of *financial leverage:* ability to borrow or increase equity in the proportion that will benefit EPS. This represents your debt-to-equity ratio also called your *capital structure.* The most important aspect of the financing decision is how your financing choice, whether you use debt, equity, or retained earnings, will affect your cash flows.

The Dividend and Stock Buyback Decision

Hopefully your investments are producing a good amount of cash that contribute to a healthy net income which can then be partially distributed as dividends to your stockholders or a stock repurchase. Recently, companies such as Apple, which last offered a dividend in 1995, announced that it would return some of its cash to shareholders in dividends and stock buybacks that will amount to $45 billion over the next three years starting in July, 2012. Apple's cash at the end of 2011 amounted to $100 billion. Even with these investments, Apple has plenty of cash to run their business and pursue strategic opportunities.[4]

The above decisions have implications for your business model. In the long term, revenues, costs, and profits tend to benefit as a result of investments guided by your business model and your value chain. From a *financial management* point of view, these three decisions contribute to your revenues and earnings, growth rates, and overall financial health.

Business Model and Financial Management Applications

To interactively learn the relationship between a business model and financial management, below are

1. Three interactive "Enter the Boardroom" applications to learn financial analysis from the key financial components of a business model.
2. One exercise to develop your financial management skills from a business model perspective.

1. Enter the Boardroom Interactive Applications

The "Enter the Boardroom" series consist of brief stories of companies to illustrate key concepts in each module. Imagine that you are an independent board member questioning decisions made by applying the concepts you learned. To be in an interactive learning environment, read each company scenario below with the corresponding concept and reflect on who should be at the table, what the agenda should consist of, and what the outcome(s) might be. This will also give you some thoughts for your own questions.

Enter the Boardroom Series: Financial Management

Google, Best Buy, Tumblr

What Is a Revenue Model? The Google Story

A revenue model is how you monetize your business model. It includes various revenue streams coming from the sale of your products or services, subscription fees, advertising fees, royalty fees, pay per use, and transaction fees. Google's revenues come mostly from Google AdWords which offers pay-per-click (PPC) advertising. Google is currently expanding their core search business to create additional revenue streams such as Google+ which is their new social networking site and Google Wallet which is their mobile-payment service.[5] (For more information on Google, read the article cited in the notes and references starting on p. 157.)

(Continued)

Enter the Google Boardroom

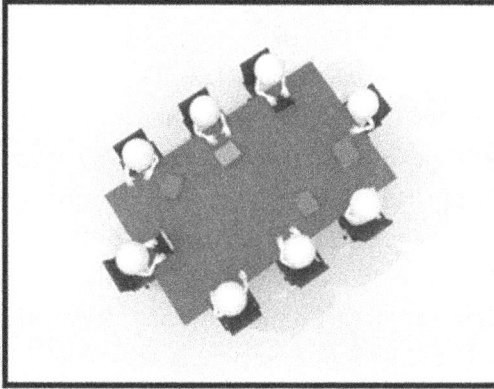

Who should be in the boardroom?
What is the agenda?
Why?

You are now a board member of Google Inc. Be prepared to answer the following questions:

1. What are Google's different revenue streams?
2. Why has Google changed its search algorithm "Penguin" and is there a revenue implication?
3. How is Google's revenue model changing and is it impacting Google's market position?

Prepare your own questions for the other members of the board:

4. What ...
5. Why ...
6. How ...
7. Other questions.

What Is a Cost Model? The Best Buy Story

A cost model refers to the cost structure of your operations. It includes the costs of making your products or delivering your services. Specifically, it includes all the costs associated with your value chain whether

(Continued)

insourced or outsourced (from raw materials to infrastructure to line and staff activities to outsourcing costs). These costs increase or decrease depending on your efficiencies, restructuring, outsourcing, and revenue growth. In the case of Best Buy, they are cutting costs by closing "big-box" stores and opening more small Best Buy Mobile outlets. In essence, they are rethinking their business model as their customers buying habits have fundamentally changed from shopping the Best Buy "showrooms" to buying online. Best Buy is struggling to reinvent itself. Some are questioning whether the management and the board realize the urgency of the situation.[6] (For more information on Best Buy, read the article cited in the notes and references starting on p. 157.)

Enter the Best Buy Boardroom

Who should be in the boardroom?
What is the agenda?
Why?

You are now a board member of Best Buy. Be prepared to answer the following questions:

1. What is an ideal cost structure for Best Buy, given its infrastructure and changing buying habits of its customers?
2. Why are Best Buy's profits declining?
3. How will Best Buy's value chain and associated costs change?

(*Continued*)

Prepare your own questions for the other members of the board:

4. What …
5. Why …
6. How …
7. Other questions.

What Is a Profit Model? The Tumblr Story

A profit model is a profit formula which includes sources of revenues, asset and process costs, economies of scale, resource velocity, and profit margins. Tumblr is a five-year-old company with 105 employees and 55 million free bloggers using its blogging platform. In the fall of 2011, it raised $85 million and was valued at $800 million. Today it is trying to make the site profitable. For the first time they are planning to sell advertising and sponsorships to fit their revenue streams to their cost structure to earn a profit and to accomplish that, they will have to develop just the right revenue model (i.e., PPC).[7] (For more information on Tumblr story, read the article cited in the notes and references starting on p. 157.)

Enter the Tumblr Boardroom

Who should be in the boardroom?
What is the agenda?
Why?

(*Continued*)

You are now a board member of Tumblr. Be prepared to answer the following questions:

1. What are the potential revenue streams for Tumblr?
2. Why has Tumblr not been profitable to date?
3. How can Tumblr generate a profit?

Prepare your own questions for the other members of the board:

4. What …
5. Why …
6. How …
7. Other questions.

2. Financial Management Scenario

This is a turnaround situation where you have to make three financial management decisions based on the business model of Best Buy. In essence, you are looking to make Best Buy financially viable in the next two years. Here is the situation:

- Declining revenues
- Declining profits
- Share price at a nine-year low
- Boardroom turmoil: Leadership exiting
- Customers are changing the way they buy electronics.

It focuses on three financial metrics: sales growth, operating margins, and net margins.

Financial Management Exercise

1. Research Best Buy Strategic Plan and Operational Plan from their 10 K (see SEC Edgar link).
2. Discuss the assumptions that Best Buy has made. Articulate the new assumptions that need to be formulated and how they could affect their value proposition.

(Continued)

3. Think of new operating metrics as key drivers. What will really drive revenue growth and earnings growth?
4. Make three financial management decisions (investment, financing, and dividend & share buyback).
5. Present recommendations as an analyst.

Guidance for the Manager:

Key Points on Financial Management

- A business model includes a revenue model, a cost model, and a profit model.
- Go deep into your metrics to discover your key drivers of performance.
- The financial health of a company is determined by looking at its strategic plan, operational plan and financial plan in addition to its financial statements.
- The assumptions of the strategic plan along with the metrics of the operational plan can result in a strong financial plan.
- The financial analysis of a business model is based on cost drivers, revenue drivers, and profit drivers.
- The revenues of a business model are best determined by buyer needs, revenue drivers, and revenue streams.
- The costs of a business model are best determined by resources and capabilities, cost drivers, and outsourcing/insourcing.
- The profits of a business model are best determined by prices, profit drivers, and gross margins, operating margins, and net margins.

Add your own key points:

Below are recommended Harvard Business Publishing cases available for purchase at: www.hbsp.harvard.edu

Nine Dragons Paper-2009
Michael Moffett; Brenda Adelson
Product Number: TB0229-PDF-ENG
Publication Date: November 16, 2010
Length: 12 pages

Description:
Nine Dragons Paper is the largest paperboard manufacturer in China and one of the largest in the world. Led by Mrs. Cheung, CEO, chairman, and founder, it has successfully grown to the top of the industry through a "grow-at-all-costs" strategy. But in the spring of 2009, the company's rising debt levels had combined with declining margins to send the company's share price tumbling. The market was increasingly worried that Mrs. Cheung's strategy was putting the company at risk.

Link to Module 2: This case provides deep insights into cost drivers of a business model.

What Happened at Citigroup? (A)
Clayton Rose; Aldo Sesia
Product Number: 310004-PDF-ENG
Publication Date: August 12, 2011
Length: 34 pages

Description:
"In 1998, the Travelers Group and Citicorp merged to create Citigroup Inc., considered the first true global "financial supermarket," and a business model to be envied, feared, and emulated. By year-end 2006 the firm had a market capitalization of $274 billion, with $1.9 trillion in assets and $24.6 billion in earnings. But 10 years after the merger it ended in tears. In July of 2009, the firm was effectively nationalized, with billions of dollars in bailout money converted into a 34% ownership stake for

the U.S. government. Citigroup was worth less than $16 billion, having lost more than $250 billion in value from its peak. This case examines Citi's business model, challenges it faced, its leadership and key decisions to better understand what contributed to the failure of one of the most powerful financial firms in the world."

Link to Module 2: This case demonstrates the financial management of a business model in the financial services industry.

Below is a recommended Harvard Business Publishing simulation available for purchase at: www.hbsp.harvard.edu

Working Capital Simulation: Managing Growth
Sandeep Dahiya
Product Number: 4302-HTM-ENG
Publication Date: July 20, 2012
Length: 60 min

Description:
"Acting as the CEO of a small company called Sunflower Nutraceuticals, students choose to invest in growth and cash-flow improvement opportunities in three phases over 10 simulated years. Examples of opportunities include taking on new customers, capitalizing on supplier discounts, and reducing inventory. Students must understand how the income statement, balance sheet, and statement of cash flows are interconnected and consider the possible effects of each opportunity on the firm's financial position. The company operates on thin margins with a constrained cash position and limited available credit. Students must optimize use of "internal" and external credit as they balance the desire for growth with the need for maintaining liquidity. This single-player simulation is ideal for introductory courses in finance, accounting, small business management, and entrepreneurial finance."

Link to Module 2: This simulation gives students an experience on how managers make financial decisions to grow a company.

Below is a recommended Harvard Business Publishing article available for purchase at: www.hbsp.harvard.edu

How to Build Risk into Your Business Model
Karan Girotra; Serguei Netessine
Product Number: R1105--PDF-ENG
Publication Date: May 01, 2011
Length: 7 pages

Description:
"To create value, companies typically focus on revenue, cost structure, and resource velocity. Improving these factors is the main focus of management literature. But all of them are vulnerable to sharp changes in demand and supply. Companies can innovate their business models to reduce the impact of such swings. But they can also create value by adding some risk. For instance, more than 30 years ago Rolls-Royce identified a major pain point in the aircraft industry: maintenance of airplane engines. An engine breakdown grounds the plane, while the airline pays for repair time and materials. So Rolls-Royce offered a service contract whereby the airline would pay for an engine's flight hours rather than for time and materials. The new contract triggered a completely new value creation dynamic, because Rolls-Royce was motivated to improve its own products and maintenance processes. Business model innovations are much cheaper than product and technology innovations, and they can be approached in a systematic way. Furthermore, nearly all the big ones have already been done so you can simply adapt them to suit your own situation."

Link to Module 2: This article reiterates the impact of market-based assumptions on potential new revenue streams.

Note: Descriptions are from www.hbsp.harvard.edu with permission.

Recommended links of various financial information and tools:

1. www.duke.edu/~charvey/Classes/wpg/glossary.htm
   Duke Professor Campbell Harvey's glossary of finance with more than 8,000 terms defined and more than 18,000 hyperlinks.

2. www.sec.gov/edgar/searchedgar/companysearch.html

   Edgar, a Securities and Exchange Commission site, contains virtually all filings of public companies in the United States. It is a treasure trove of financial information, including annual and quarterly reports.

3. www.berkshirehathaway.com

   Find more Warren Buffet's legendary letters to shareholders as well as Buffet's "Owner's Manual." In his 2011 letter to shareholders he talks about "intrinsic business value."

4. www.vnpartners.com

   This site has an informative primer on venture capital taking an idea to an initial public offering business model.

5. www.valuepro.net

   This site is a free discounted cash flow valuation model based on 20 input variables. Enter a stock ticker symbol and ValuePro values the business based on current estimates of the 20 variables. Change the variables and the estimated stock price changes. Check to see if your stocks are overpriced, underpriced, or priced just right.

Reflect on what you originally included on the first page of this module and how your understanding of the relationships of the components of a business model to financial management has changed. Are you ready to rethink your approach to financial management and take action?

MODULE 3

Business Model and Strategic Direction

Taking the square to a new dimension, we will examine those components that will give your business model a strategic direction. We use the geometric form of a diamond to demonstrate the interrelationships of the elements of strategic direction to the business model.

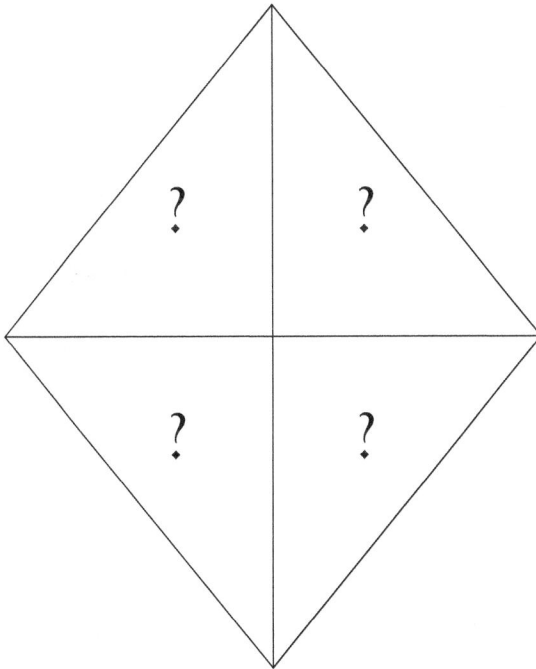

In your view, what does it take to set a strategic direction once you have a good business model? Use the diamond shape above to think of four core elements that represent your concept of a strategic direction before going to the next page.

Imagine a purple diamond to reflect on a meaningful purpose

Objectives

1. Understand the concept of strategic direction.
2. Use real-world examples of companies' strategic directions.
3. Discuss strategic decisions.

Prelude

Poor management, lack of investment, inability to adapt to new market conditions, lack of direction, unsustainable business model; you've heard them all before. Every day the popular media reports numerous examples of companies that do not have meaningful strategic direction from the leadership. A current example of a company that is reestablishing its strategic direction is Yahoo! Externally, the company faces formidable industry dynamics with Facebook and Google as key players. Internally, the leadership wants to refocus on a new vision, restructure the executive team, and reconsider the broader questions of what kind of company Yahoo! should be. Its strategy has shifted under changing leadership and many investors wonder what the company's direction will be. They are rethinking investment in specialized technology such as "right media exchange" and whether certain partnerships and acquisitions make strategic and financial sense.[1] One recent CEO Scott Thompson stated that he was "looking widely across Yahoo! in order to jump-start what largely has been a failed turnaround for the company under previous leadership. We will do more than protect our current revenue streams," he said. "We will consider new business models and revenue sources." A Yahoo! spokesperson said, "Our leadership is engaged in a process that will generate significant strategic change at Yahoo!, but final decisions have not yet been made at this point."[2] So a new CEO was announced, Marissa Mayer, who has deep technology experience, given her tenure at Google. She expressed that the main revenue source will continue to be advertising and that she will inject some innovation and new ways of advertising into its business model.[3] However, analysts are not sure whether "the strategic direction is going to change from what was previously articulated as refocusing Yahoo! on its online-ad business."[4]

There are many definitions of leadership and the practice of leadership varies from leader to leader as well. However, it is well known that the purpose of leadership is to strategically manage an organization by setting a strategic direction. It is also interesting to note that academic studies are advancing the notion of strategic direction by incorporating sustainability concepts into the development of business models which impacts setting company direction, such as shaping the mission or becoming the driving force of the firm and its decision making.[5] This module focuses on the core elements of setting a strategic direction for a business model-centric organization.

Characteristics of a Sound Strategic Direction

The previous two modules focused on what it takes to build a sound business model. Once you have a promising business model, lead it into the future with the right strategic direction. There are four core elements of setting a company's strategic direction: a company's strategic vision, business mission, performance objectives, and its strategies.

Let's use a metaphor to see the link between a business model and a strategic direction.

The business model is the internal engine where the operating parts (operations, processes, and systems) fit together. The strategic direction provides the fuel to keep it running and the lubrication for needed adjustments.

Because we are discussing setting a strategic direction to compete well, it is imperative to first point out what constitutes a strategic decision, and what matters strategically in terms of competition and industry from the perspective of a business model.

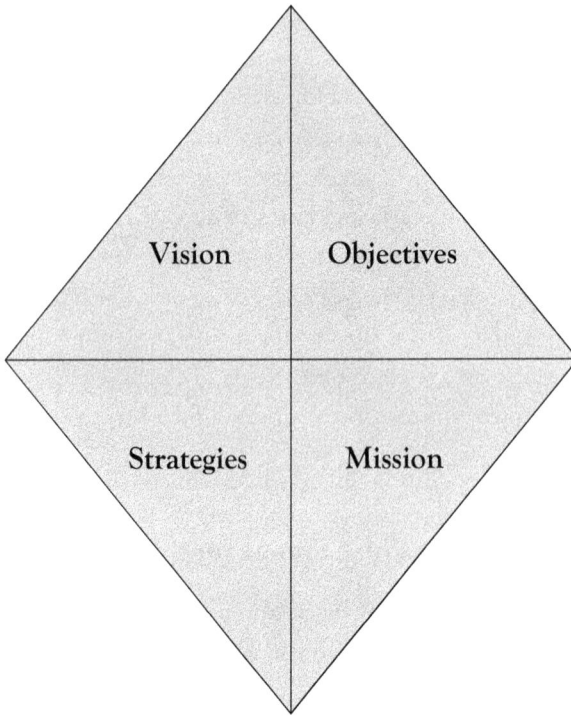

Figure 3. Components of a strategic direction.

Making Strategic Decisions

Obviously setting a strategic direction involves making strategic decisions. Therefore, it is important to understand what a strategic decision is. Let's begin with what makes a decision strategic. More specifically, a decision is strategic when it leads a company into a new business area, changes the future direction of the firm, affects the firm as a whole, has a significant financial impact on the firm, and can result in a significant response from competitors or other stakeholders. In other words, it is strategic if it impacts your company's business model, its future direction, and its competitors.

Assessing the Competition

The traditional view of competitive analysis to provide information and data to set a strategic direction is to understand your strengths and weaknesses vis-à-vis your competitors and discover their competitive advantages or vulnerabilities. From a business model point of view, the critical areas to understand revolve around the difficulty of recognizing market shifts. Those include having a grasp of the assumptions that are being made about the market, understanding the competitors' positions on the potential to create a market shift, and realizing the conditions that exist to make competitors move industries in a certain direction.

If a competitive analysis addresses those areas, you will be in a much better position to make the right assumptions in order to create the market shift and move your industry with your business model.

Understanding the Industry Dynamics

The most famous framework to understand industry dynamics remains Michael Porter's seminal Five Forces article.[6] Let's interpret it as it applies to a business model. Looking at the five competitive forces—threat of new entrants, bargaining power of suppliers, bargaining power of customers, rivalry among competitors, and threat of substitutes—will give you insight into the drivers of competition in your industry to help you understand what influences profitability in order to develop strategies to enhance the long-term profitability of your business model.

Developing a Strategic Vision

Former IBM CEO, Louis V. Gerstner, once said that the time to set a vision is when you need a new strategic direction. Management's most important job is not to see the company as it is but rather as what it can become. Employees of Yahoo! "need a vision to rally around and a leader they believe can take them there."[7] The first task of the new CEO will be to articulate a vision. Setting a strategic vision is finding your company's identity that will stay relevant based on your company's core values and business model. Your company's core identity is nurtured by knowing your company's milestone accomplishments, your company's dynamic capabilities, and your company's capacity to change.

The most famous example of a strategic vision is Steve Jobs in the beginning stages of what later became Apple Inc. His vision for Apple was that of having a computer in every home. You could say that this was Apple's core ideology, *raison d'être,* identity, and relevance. It seems that the vision came first because of its "visionary" leader. Then over time as Apple developed as an organization it defined its mission, objectives, and strategies and refined its business model.

Defining a Business Mission

As the boundaries of industries are blurring, it is helpful to define your mission by refocusing on the business(es) or business arena you are in or wish to be in and the level of integration you can realistically achieve based on your business model—a fully integrated firm, partially integrated, or a specialized firm. A good mission statement is unique, specific to your business model and helps to make strategic choices.

The mission of Apple today is *"Apple designs Macs, the best personal computers in the world, along with OS X, iLife, iWork and professional software. Apple leads the digital music revolution with its iPods and iTunes online store. Apple has reinvented the mobile phone with its revolutionary iPhone and App Store, and is defining the future of mobile media and computing devices with iPad."*[8]

So Apple designs, leads, and reinvents. Apple is a fully integrated organization from manufacturing to retailing.

Setting Performance Objectives

A performance objective is a specific, measurable, and attainable performance target to be achieved within a specific period. In the realm of setting a strategic direction, your objectives are a direct conduit to your company performance assuming the right strategies. As we saw in the previous section, your business model will determine your strategy. Now let's look at the results you want to achieve with your strategy. There are two important types of results: financial performance and strategic performance. Both are essential to sustain your business model.

The achievement of strategic and financial objectives will determine whether your company needs a new set of objectives. Having a clear vision of why a company exists and what it can become as well as knowing how it can best compete with its business model is the starting point of setting good financial and performance objectives. Those objectives can turn into progress milestones, build dynamic capabilities, and enhance your company's capacity to change. Setting and achieving those objectives will keep your business model relevant.

Creating a Strategy

Strategy is developed at the corporate level, the competitive level (also known as the business level), and the operational level (also known as the functional level). Each level is addressed in Module 5. In this module we focus on the competitive level because your business model significantly influences how you compete. Your company's ability to compete with a strategy depends on the nature of your industry and your business model. You have basically two choices of competitive strategies: low-cost or differentiation strategies. Your business model will either enhance or impede your company's capacity to compete. In addition, you need to pay attention to particular areas of your company to use these strategies effectively. Creating and pursuing a low-cost strategy requires capabilities and or investments in the following:

- Manufacturing capabilities (do you have enough scale capacity?)
- Process efficiencies (can you achieve economies?)
- Market share building (have you been growing your revenues and market share?)

Creating and pursuing a differentiation strategy requires investments in the following:

- Marketing capabilities (are you able to strengthen your product and market positions?)
- Research and development (what is guiding your R&D focus?)
- Product innovation (are you known for your product innovations?)

Business Model and Strategic Direction Applications

To interactively learn the relationship between a business model and strategic direction, below are

1. Three interactive "Enter the Boardroom" applications to learn how the strategic direction of companies affects the success of their business model.
2. One exercise to develop your strategic thinking skills from a business model perspective.

1. Enter the Boardroom Interactive Applications

The "Enter the Boardroom" series consist of brief stories of companies to illustrate key concepts in each module. Imagine that you are an independent board member questioning decisions made by applying the concepts you learned. To be in an interactive learning environment, read each company scenario below with the corresponding concept and reflect on who should be at the table, what the agenda should consist of, and what the outcome(s) might be. This will also give you some thoughts for your own questions.

Enter the Boardroom Series: Strategic Direction

Yahoo!, Nike, Nokia

What Is a Strategic Vision? The Yahoo! Story

A strategic vision is the macro view of what your company can become. It is based on your company's *raison d'être,* its core purpose, its relevance, its consistent identity, its core values, and core ideology. The role of a strategic vision is to inspire and guide decision making. A strategic vision takes shape by knowing your business model well, knowing your core values, and knowing what will keep your company relevant.

(Continued)

As discussed in the Prelude section, the Yahoo! story is about a company that either ignored or did not have a strategic vision. For example, in 2006, Yahoo! wanted to buy Facebook for a little more than $1 billion. In 2008, Yahoo! was almost acquired by Microsoft for more than $40 billion. How did either of these fit into Yahoo!'s strategic vision? Yahoo!'s performance has been declining. Now Yahoo! is trying to make a turnaround and establish a strategic direction under new leadership.[9] (For more information on Yahoo!, read the article cited in the notes and references starting on p. 157.)

Enter the Yahoo! Boardroom

Who should be in the boardroom?
What is the agenda?
Why?

You are now a board member of Yahoo! Be prepared to answer the following questions:

1. What is Yahoo!'s strategic vision? What are Yahoo!'s core values and identity?
2. Why did it cease to compete well?
3. How will Yahoo! stay relevant?

(*Continued*)

Prepare your own questions for the other members of the board:

4. What …
5. Why …
6. How …
7. Other questions.

What Is a Business Mission? The Nike Story

The fundamental question that sustains organizations is 'What is our business?' In other words, defining a mission is looking at what you do that customers buy and why they are buying from you. Consider these questions to help define a mission statement that reflects customers' enthusiasm for your products or services and the essence of your organization (how you create and deliver value to your customers and satisfy their needs).

Nike is in the business of designing, marketing, and distributing athletic shoes and apparels. Their business does not include the manufacturing of their designs. They have a global outsourcing network of manufacturers that operate under a Nike license to make Nike products for Nike. Part of Nike's business model is to achieve cost savings by not having to invest heavily in manufacturing. Rather, their previous mission focused them on investing in dynamic design processes and distribution capabilities keeping their business model sustainable. Their new mission captures their customers' enthusiasm for their products and the Nike essence stated as "to bring inspiration and innovation to every athlete in the world …" If you have a body, you are an athlete. When Nike co-founder Bill Bowerman made this observation many years ago, he was defining how he viewed the endless possibilities for human potential in sports.[10] (For more information on Nike, read the article cited in the notes and references starting on p. 157.)

(Continued)

Enter the Nike Boardroom

Who should be in the boardroom?
What is the agenda?
Why?

You are now a board member of Nike. Be prepared to answer the following questions:

1. What growth opportunities are you envisioning based on your mission?
2. Why is Nike not fully integrated?
3. How is Nike using its mission to enhance its business model?

Prepare your own questions for the other members of the board:

4. What ...
5. Why ...
6. How ...
7. Other questions.

(Continued)

What Are Strategic and Financial Objectives and the Strategies to Achieve Them? The Nokia Story

Nokia's mission is simple: "Connecting People." From this mission, their goal is to build great mobile products that enable billions of people worldwide to enjoy more of what life has to offer. Their challenge is to achieve this in an increasingly dynamic and competitive environment.

Nokia's strategic objective is to "regain leadership in the smart-phone space. To help us achieve our mission, Nokia has formed a strategic partnership with Microsoft that will, we hope, see us regain lost ground in the smartphone market."

Nokia's strategy is "to leverage its innovation and strength in growth markets to connect even more people to their first Internet and application experience. To drive change, Nokia's new strategy is supported by changes in Nokia's leadership, operational structure, and approach. The renewed governance will expedite decision-making and improve time-to-market of products and innovations, placing a heavy focus on results, speed and accountability."[11] (For more information on Nokia, read the article cited in the notes and references starting on p. 157.)

Enter the Nokia Boardroom

Who should be in the boardroom?
What is the agenda?
Why?

(*Continued*)

You are now a board member of Nokia. Be prepared to answer the following questions:

1. What are Nokia's strategic and financial objectives?
2. Why has Nokia "lost ground"?
3. How does Nokia's strategy differ from its competitors in the smart phone business?

Prepare your own questions for the other members of the board:

1. What …
2. Why …
3. How …
4. Other questions.

2. Strategic Direction Analysis Exercise

Toys "R" Us is seeking your advice to reinvent itself! Toys "R" Us is the last of the big toy stores. Wal-Mart and Amazon are eating away at their market share. There is a market shift going on. Toys "R" Us strategies have included the following:

1. Increasing private labels and exclusive toys (e.g., F.A.O. Schwarz), which now represent 50% of their toy sales, and that no one else can offer.
2. Combining Toys "R" Us and Babies "R" Us stores.
3. Adding 600 pop-up stores in 2010 for the Christmas season.
4. Increasing Internet sales.
5. Increasing international stores.

Toys "R" Us has $5.2 billion in debt, weak financial results, and leadership is leaving.[12]

Strategic Direction Exercise

1. Conduct the Q and V tests (see module one for guidance on these tests) on the toy industry and the Toys "R" Us business model.
   - Q (quantitative): provide three yr trend data in sales growth %, operating margin %, net profit margin % for Toys "R" Us and for the retail toy industry(use industry % as base % to draw conclusions).
   - V (value): describe their value proposition, strategic resources, dynamic capabilities, and the industry dynamics.
2. From the discussion of assumptions in Module 2 on Financial Management, discuss the assumptions that Toys "R" Us has made. Articulate the new assumptions that need to be formulated and how it is affecting their value proposition.
3. From the discussion of metrics in Module 2 on Financial Management, think of new operating metrics as key drivers. What will really drive revenue growth and earnings growth?
4. Based on the above tests, assumptions and metrics, set a new vision, mission, performance objectives and strategies that will give Toys "R" Us a new strategic direction.
5. Present recommendations as an analyst.

Guidance for the Manager:

Key Points on Strategic Direction

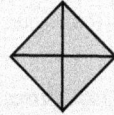

- Setting a strategic direction includes a strategic vision, a business mission, a set of strategic and financial objectives, and a competitive strategy.
- Setting a new strategic direction involves making **strategic decisions** which affect your business model, your company's future direction, and your competitors.
- Both are dependent on your company's **capacity to change**.

A strategic vision reflects the core ideology which consists of what a company stands for (its core values), why a company exists (its core purpose—raison d'etre), and what it aspires to be. The role of a core ideology is to guide and inspire.

A business mission is who we are, what we do, and where we are now. It aslo captures the scope of the firm as fully integrated, partially integrated, or a specialized firm.

Strategic objectives address the long-term market position and competitiveness of a company. Financial objectives target efficiency and effectiveness areas with ratios such ROE, ROA, ROI, ROS (net profit margin).

A strategy is to help your company compete using its business model. The success of a low-cost or differentiation competitive strategy is based on how you use your resources, capabilities, and competencies in your operations.

Add your own key points:

Below are recommended Harvard Business Publishing cases available for purchase at: www.hbsp.harvard.edu

Case: Crocs (B): Hitting the Skids
Michael Marks; Hau Lee; David W. Hoyt
Product Number: GS57B-PDF-ENG
Publication Date: March 07, 2011
Length: 4 pages

Description:
Through 2007, Crocs grew rapidly, and its stock soared. In early 2008, the stock plunged, as analysts cited excess inventory. During 2008, revenues decreased, and the company restructured. The B case summarizes these developments, and asks what the company should do now.

Link to Module 3: This case lends itself nicely to setting a strategic direction for the Crocs business model which is based on a reconfigured and somewhat revolutionary supply chain.

Case: Organization and Strategy at Millennium (B)
Julie M. Wulf; Scott Waggoner
Product Number: 710418-PDF-ENG
Publication Date: February 02, 2010
Length: 11 pages

Description:
"This case examines Millennium's strategic and organizational responses to the rapid evolution of the biopharmaceutical industry. In the early 2000s, as Millennium's competitive advantage in early-stage research slipped away and its losses mounted, founder–CEO Mark Levin moved the firm downstream away from research and toward drug development and commercialization, while narrowing horizontal breadth from over a dozen therapeutic classes to just three. In 2005, Levin hired Deborah Dunsire from Novartis as CEO to lead Millennium's continuing transformation. Students are asked to put themselves in the shoes of incoming CEO Dunsire and to provide organizational recommendations to execute the new strategy."

Link to Module 3: This case provides insight into how to execute a strategy as one of the four elements of setting and pursuing a strategic direction.

Below are recommended Harvard Business Publishing articles available for purchase at: www.hbsp.harvard.edu

The Five Competitive Forces That Shape Strategy
Michael E. Porter
Product Number: R0801E-PDF-ENG
Publication Date: January 01, 2008
Length: 19 pages

Description:
"This article includes a one-page preview that quickly summarizes the key ideas and provides an overview of how the concepts work in practice along with suggestions for further reading.

In 1979, a young associate professor at Harvard Business School published his first article for HBR, *How Competitive Forces Shape Strategy.* In the years that followed, Michael Porter's explication of the five forces that determine the long-run profitability of any industry has shaped a generation of academic research and business practice. In this article, Porter undertakes a thorough reaffirmation and extension of his classic work of strategy formulation, which includes substantial new sections showing how to put the five forces analysis into practice. The five forces govern the profit structure of an industry by determining how the economic value it creates is apportioned. That value may be drained away through the rivalry among existing competitors, of course, but it can also be bargained away through the power of suppliers or the power of customers or be constrained by the threat of new entrants or the threat of substitutes. Strategy can be viewed as building defenses against the competitive forces or as finding a position in an industry where the forces are weaker. Changes in the strength of the forces signal changes in the competitive landscape critical to ongoing strategy formulation. In exploring the implications of the five forces framework, Porter explains why a fast-growing industry is not always a profitable one, how eliminating today's competitors through mergers and acquisitions can reduce an industry's profit potential, how government policies play a role by changing the relative strength of the forces, and how to use the forces to understand complements. He then shows how a company can influence the key forces in its industry to create a more favorable structure for itself or to expand the pie altogether. The five forces reveal why industry profitability is what it is. Only by understanding them can a company incorporate industry conditions into strategy."

Link to Module 3: This article provides insight into industry conditions (dynamics) as the drivers of competition to rethink a business model.

How to Make the Most of Your Company's Strategy
Stephen Bungay
Product Number: R1101L-PDF-ENG
Publication Date: January 01, 2011
Length: 10 pages

Description:
"Corporate strategy often seems abstract to managers on the ground, who struggle to translate it into a realistic plan of action. But a process called strategy briefing, which originated with the military, can help them overcome that challenge. Bungay, the director of the Ashridge Strategic Management Centre, describes in this article how briefings can move managers and their reports from confusion about a complex set of goals and performance measures to clarity about just which objectives each person needs to focus on and in what order. Using a fictional case study as an illustration, Bungay outlines the five critical steps of the process: (1) state your intent, or what you are expected to do and why, (2) revise it in the context of your company's situation, (3) determine which measures indicate whether you're achieving your goal, (4) define the tasks implied by your intent, and (5) define the boundaries, or constraints, that limit your team. A single strategy briefing can help a team perform better, but the real magic happens when briefings roll down through an entire organization. When that occurs, the company's strategy is broken into a cascade of discrete but linked elements. In the end, people will be strategically

aligned and operationally autonomous—a combination that is one of the hallmarks of high-performance organizations."

Link to Module 3: This article helps to set meaningful goals and understand the difference between strategy and business model.

The CEO's Role in Business Model Reinvention
Vijay Govindarajan; Chris Trimble
Product Number: R1101H-PDF-ENG
Publication Date: January 01, 2011
Length: 8 pages

Description:

"Fending off new competitors is a perennial struggle for established companies. Govindarajan and Trimble, of Dartmouth's Tuck School of Business, explain why: Many corporations become too comfortable with their existing business models and neglect the necessary work of radically reinventing them. The authors map out an alternative in their "three boxes" framework. They argue that while a CEO manages the present (box 1), he or she must also selectively forget the past (box 2) in order to create the future (box 3). Infosys chairman N.R. Narayana Murthy mastered the three boxes to reinvigorate his company and greatly increased its chances of enduring for generations."

Link to Module 3: This article shows how to use business models as a source for a strategic vision.

Note: Descriptions are from www.hbsp.harvard.edu with permission.

Reflect on what you originally included on the first page of this module and how your understanding of the relationship between a business model and strategic direction has changed. Are you ready to rethink your strategic direction and take action?

MODULE 4

Business Model and Competitive Advantage

We have chosen the circle as our geometric form because it constitutes a target for the elements that are necessary to focus our business model on ensuring a sustainable competitive advantage.

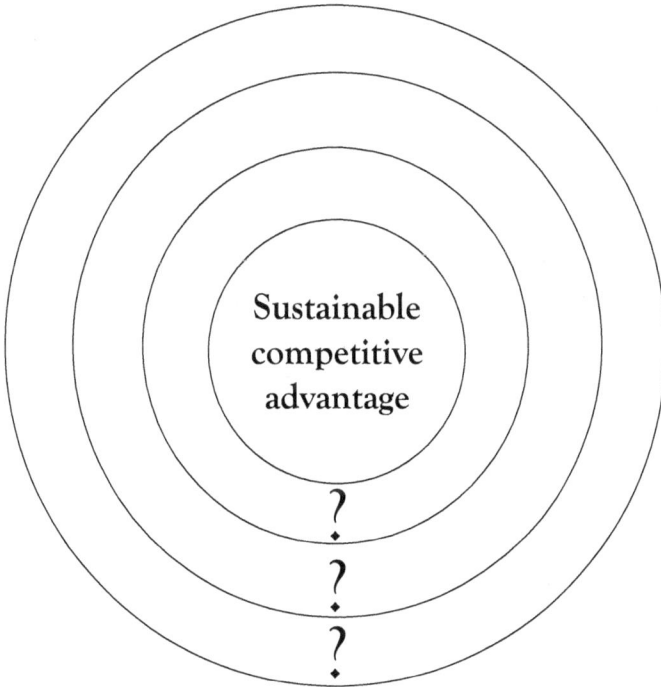

In your view, what does it take to develop a competitive advantage once you have a good business model? Use the circle shapes above to think of three core elements with which you can build a foundation for ensuring competitive advantage, before going to the next page.

Imagine a red circle in the middle to focus on the sustainability of a competitive advantage

Objectives

1. Understand the concept of a business model-based competency.
2. Use real-world examples of companies' competencies.
3. Discuss competency decisions.

Prelude

France 1759, the Age of Reason, the Year of Grace, Voltaire publishes Candide at the age of 65. When I think of this philosophical novel, I think about Candide who says "let us cultivate our garden" or *il faut finir par cultiver son jardin.*[1] A beautiful garden is the result of constant nurturing. You keep looking at it and hope that its beauty evolves from a lot of care such as proper seeding, planting, fertilizing, watering, weeding, pruning, and growing. Mending your garden is like mending the vision for your organization. It requires new ideas (seeding), new projects or acquisitions (planting), R&D investments (fertilizing), nurturing resources and capabilities (watering), streamlining (weeding), restructuring (pruning), and implementing the vision (growing). In the previous module we talked about developing a strategic vision by knowing your business model (what is making your company successful now), your core values, and how to keep your company relevant. Company relevance is achieved by knowing its milestones, its dynamic capabilities, and its capacity to change. In this module we focus on how nurturing your strategic resources can build dynamic capabilities into competencies as a foundation for growth.

In 1995, I wrote my dissertation on resource-based global alliances as determinants of strategic capabilities. I surveyed 38 global companies on the types of resources that were put into a total of 480 global alliances and looked to see whether it contributed to their strategic capabilities over time. I found that it did when companies contributed firm-specific resources to the alliance (i.e., strategic resources). By combining strategic resources—organizational resources, technological resources, and physical resources—dynamic capabilities were developed in engineering and systems innovation, production and information technology, distribution, product and process R&D, and general management. A recent academic study shows that technology partnerships develop R&D capabilities that are critical for business model innovation (see Appendix B).

Some competitors of equal standing are more profitable than others in the same industry. The difference is attributed to how well they use strategic resources and capabilities to support their business model. Capabilities are based on strategic resources, combined in such a way as to create a dynamic capability which results in unique processes conducive to a core competency often defined as a real proficiency area most important to the performance of the business model. Capabilities are anything an organization does well that drives meaningful business results.

Characteristics of a Sound Core Competency

Depending on the business model, the financial management, and the strategic direction, each company combines its resources differently to develop strong capabilities and processes that can become core competencies. The resource-based view sees companies as having a collection of assets used as resources and capabilities to develop some unique competencies. Building on that, the business model view sees companies as developing competencies that are essential to the value proposition and the profit formula. So if the value proposition is to "have news 24/7" (CNN), what resources and capabilities do we need to make this idea financially viable? How different from the traditional broadcasting companies (i.e., ABC, CBS, NBC) do we need to be in how we use our resources to generate dynamic capabilities and processes to create the competencies that will support our business model and gain a sustainable competitive advantage?

The relationship between your business model and your competencies lies in your capacity to identify the strategic resources with which to build dynamic processes resulting in the right competencies to deliver the value proposition.

This module presents a dynamic-capabilities approach to building the competency(ies) needed to support a business model. The business model view shows how a firm can operate profitably based on its competencies. The test of a competency is its alignment to the value proposition.

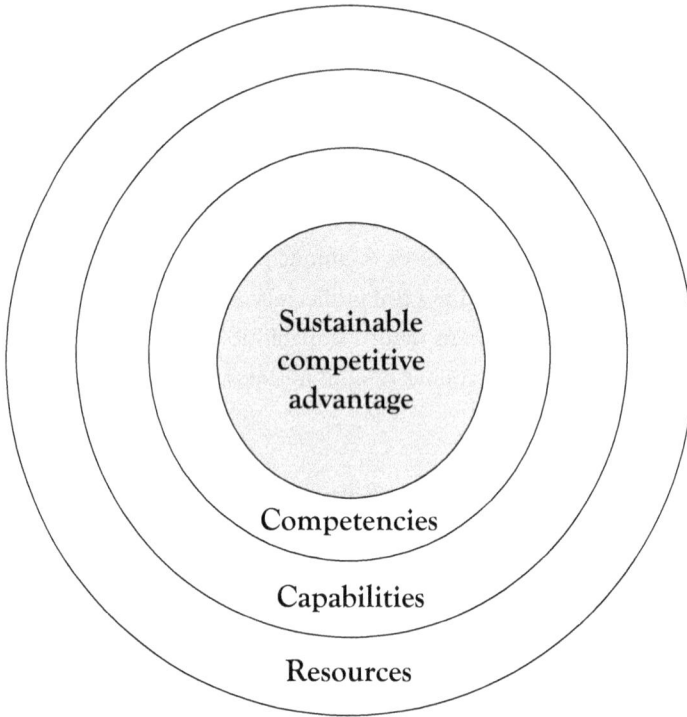

Figure 4. Components of competitive advantage.

Dynamic Capabilities and Competencies

The diagram for this module is a set of circles with a target precision overlay. It conveys gradual alignment of resources into capabilities, capabilities into competencies, and the use of this competency foundation to achieve the target of a competitive advantage which, optimally, should be sustainable.

And then there is the question of the dynamic nature of your processes or capabilities. Dynamic capabilities are fundamentally the organization's capacity to effectively reconfigure the use of its strategic resources to successfully implement its strategies and achieve a competitive advantage. The strategic imperative when it comes to a dynamic capability is not leverage but change.[2] Once you have a dynamic capability that meets the criteria of value, rareness, and inimitability, you have a competency. Teece et al. (1997) define dynamic capabilities as an organization's ability to reconfigure internal and external competencies to address rapidly changing environments and to achieve innovative forms of competitive advantage.[3] Finding your strategic resources, developing your dynamic capabilities, and building unique competencies will keep your business model relevant.

Competitive Advantage

Although the diagram for this module points to the ultimate goal of developing a sustainable competitive advantage, the essence of the module is about having the right mix of resources to create dynamic capabilities in order to develop competencies. It is presented here as a way to link it to the next module on strategy. In that context, the link between your dynamic capabilities and competencies, and your competitive advantage is by choosing the right strategy for your business model. For example, if you have a competency in inventory management like Wal-Mart you can compete very well with a low-cost strategy and develop a competitive advantage as a result. Module 5—Business Model and Strategy—will cover this aspect in depth including how to assess that you indeed have a competitive advantage. "Building core competencies, resource strengths, and organizational capabilities that rivals can't match is a sound foundation for sustainable competitive advantage."[4]

Strategic Alliances

A pertinent example of dynamic capabilities and competencies involves adding to your strategic resources with strategic alliances. I did a meta-analysis study to provide evidence on how alliance capability becomes dynamic and develops strategies to compete globally. An alliance capability is the capacity of an organization to extend or modify its resource base by accessing a combined mix of resources from alliance partners. A dynamic alliance capability is built from processes in organizational learning mechanisms, (how and where you learn from your alliance experiences), alliance management, (how and where you integrate, diffuse the knowledge and reconfigure resources), and strategic review and alignment, (how and where you assess the contributions of your alliances to your business model). If these processes are in place, you in fact are developing a dynamic capability that can become a competency for your organization and add value.

Value Chain and the Business Model

To build real value in your business model, you need to build capabilities and competencies. The most important tool that can help you determine whether or not you should be developing or strengthening your competencies is the Porter's value chain. It is directly related to the use of resources, capabilities, and competencies to add value to your operations, to your end products or services, to your quality, and to your customer satisfaction. The rule of thumb is when you find that another company can do the job better and faster, outsource it to them because you are losing value by doing it yourself. If you have a fully integrated company, then your value comes from the integration of all your parts. If, for example, investing in your own distribution system will not add value to the efficiency of your operations, then the best strategic step is to outsource.

Both your value chain and your business model help you understand how your competencies affect costs, add value, and contribute to your profitability. It is also a framework that ties together all the strategic resources and capabilities you should invest in given your business model. This also makes you understand what resources, capabilities, and competencies are competitively relevant.

Business Model and Competitive Advantage Applications

To interactively learn the relationship between the business model and the competitive advantage, below are

1. Three interactive "Enter the Boardroom" applications to learn how the key components of a business model can lead to a competitive advantage.
2. One exercise to develop how the strategic resources, dynamic capabilities and competencies are essential to support the impact of the business model.

1. *Enter the Boardroom Interactive Applications*

The "Enter the Boardroom" series consist of brief stories of companies to illustrate key concepts in each module. Imagine that you are an independent board member questioning decisions made by applying the concepts you learned. To be in an interactive learning environment, read each company scenario below with the corresponding concept and reflect on who should be at the table, what the agenda should consist of, and what the outcome(s) might be. This will also give you some thoughts for your own questions.

Enter the Boardroom Series: Competencies

Microsoft, Avon, and Samsung

What Is a Strategic Resource? The Microsoft Story

It is a strategic asset. There are five categories of resources: human (skills and knowledge of your employees), financial (cash, receivables), physical (plant and equipment), organizational (supplier networks, market research results, intellectual property), and technological (databases, technology, patents). When companies use their assets strategically to develop capabilities and competencies to impact the performance of their business models, they have strategic resources. In other words, understanding your business model drives your ability to develop assets into strategic resources.

Microsoft is buying a collection of patents as strategic assets. AOL has agreed to sell Microsoft about 1,100 patents for nearly $1.1 billion. They are called "strategic financial assets." Examples include 142 patents on prioritizing online messages, and 81 patents on directing a browser request.[5] (For more information on Microsoft, read the article cited in the notes and references starting on p. 157.)

(Continued)

Enter the Microsoft Boardroom

Who should be in the boardroom?
What is the agenda?
Why?

You are now a board member of Microsoft. Be prepared to answer the following questions:

1. What is the strategic value of those patents for Microsoft's business model?
2. Why pay a premium?
3. How will those patents evolve into revenue streams?

Prepare your own questions for the other members of the board:

4. What …
5. Why …
6. How …
7. Other questions.

(*Continued*)

What Is a Dynamic Capability? The Avon Story

Strategic resources used in the right mix are called dynamic capabilities or processes. It is dynamic because the resources are unique and capable of adapting, reacting, or advancing a process in a sustainable way. For example, having the right employee talent pool represents a strategic asset. When used with the company's advanced technologies, efficient infrastructure, and managerial practices it can lead to a dynamic capability.

One of Avon's dynamic capabilities has been its direct-sales capability. It now has a new CEO, Sherilyn S. McCoy, whose most important task is to develop a strategic plan to include a rethinking of its capabilities while fending off an unwanted $10 billion takeover offer.[6] (For more information on Avon, read the article cited in the notes and references starting on p. 157.)

Enter the Avon Boardroom

Who should be in the boardroom?
What is the agenda?
Why?

(Continued)

You are now a board member of Avon Products Inc. Be prepared to answer the following questions:

1. What do you consider your most important strategic resources are?
2. Why is Avon fighting a $10 billion takeover by Coty?
3. How can Avon develop new dynamic capabilities?

Prepare your own questions for the other members of the board:

4. What ...
5. Why ...
6. How ...
7. Other questions.

What Is a Competency? The Samsung Electronics Story

A dynamic capability can become a competency when it passes the VRIO test which helps to determine whether a capability inherently possesses four characteristics. This is how we look at those characteristics from a business model view:

Valuable: Is the capability essential to the value proposition in a cost-effective way?

Rare: Is it unique to your firm?

Imitability: Is it costly to imitate?

Organization: Is it dynamic (sustainable and adaptable)?

Responding yes to at least three of the above questions makes your capability a true competency for delivering value to your business model.

Samsung is "the world's biggest technology company by revenue." Their capacity to change was evident with its fast transition from cellphones to smartphones. Samsung's cellphone/smartphone division is "the company's largest by revenue." It is using its dynamic capabilities from its chip division to quickly achieve a changeover and become the leader in smartphones.[7] (For more information on Samsung, read the article cited in the notes and references starting on p. 157.)

(Continued)

Enter the Samsung Boardroom

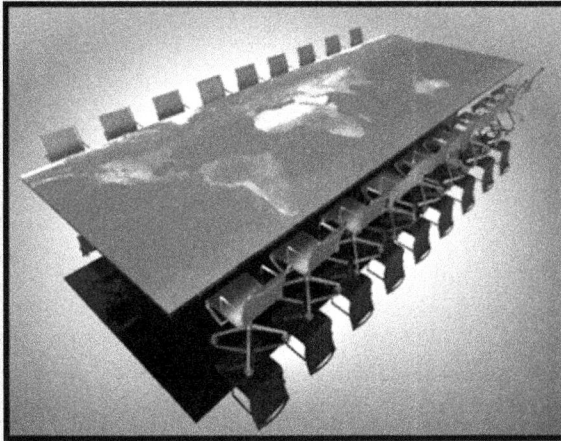

Who should be in the boardroom?
What is the agenda?
Why?

You are now a board member of Samsung Electronics Co. Be prepared to answer the following questions:

1. What is Samsung's distinctive competency that contributes the most value to its business model?
2. Why is Samsung's performance increasing?
3. How does Samsung sustain its capacity to change as a competency?

Prepare your own questions for the other members of the board:

4. What ...
5. Why ...
6. How ...
7. Other questions.

To recap, using the business model, the value chain, and the VRIO framework can help identify the strategic resources areas, the capabilities, and the competencies in the value chain and their linkages

(Continued)

to business model performance. For example, Amazon has a strategic resources area in distribution. They have strategic assets in modern warehousing technologies, robots, systems, and a well-trained work force. Together those resources create dynamic capabilities and, over time, build competencies in distribution that are essential to executing their business model successfully.

2. Competency Analysis

We have talked about how to view an organization in terms of its strategic resources to develop dynamic capabilities and competencies to impact its business model profitability. The example we will use for this analysis is Google. Google's mission is "to organize the world's information and make it universally accessible and useful." Their "unexpressed commercial mission is to monetize consumers' intentions as revealed by their searches and other online behavior."[8]

- Google is No. 1 in web-search engines.
- Google has a 10-year-old shopping site which competes with Amazon and eBay.
- On June 1, 2012, Google started to charge online retailers to display their products on Google's shopping site where it used to be free.

Competency Analysis

1. Will this require Google to develop or acquire new strategic resources, dynamic capabilities and core competency?
2. Conduct the following competency analysis test: (use the matrix on the next page)

   - Identify three key Google strategic resource areas.
   - Identify three dynamic capabilities (one per strategic resource area).
   - Identify Google's competencies using the VRIO characteristics.

3. Based on the above test, comment as to whether or not Google has the competency foundation to better compete in shopping-related searches.
4. Discuss the negative or positive impact of their competencies on their business model.
5. Present recommendations as an analyst.

Strategic Assets/ Resource Areas:	Dynamic Capabilities:	VRIO:	Competen-cies:	Business Model Impact: + or −

Guidance for the Manager:

Key Points on Competitive Advantage

- A competitive advantage is built on business model-capabilities.
- Capabilities are developed from strategic resources.
- A strategic resource is a strategic asset used to develop capabilities in a company's value chain.
- A dynamic process is the right mix of strategic resources to build capabilities and competencies.
- Use dynamic processes to develop competencies that support a unique business model to result in a competitive advantage.

Add your own key points:

Below are recommended Harvard Business Publishing cases available for purchase at: www.hbsp.harvard.edu

Crocs: Revolutionizing an Industry's Supply Chain Model for Competitive Advantage

Michael Marks; Chuck Holloway; Hau Lee;
David W. Hoyt; Amanda Silverman
Product Number: GS57-PDF-ENG
Revision Date: March 07, 2011
Publication Date: June 18, 2007
Length: 22 pages

Description:

"This case discusses the astounding growth of Crocs Inc., a manufacturer of plastic shoes, from 2003 through early 2007. Much of the company's growth was made possible by a highly flexible supply chain that enabled Crocs to build additional product within the selling season. The normal model used within the fashion industry was to take orders well in advance of each selling season, and produce to those orders, with relatively little additional production. If demand was far in excess of this production, there would be stockouts and the company would lose the ability to capture revenue for that season. The product might or might not be in fashion the following year, when production would again be based on preseason orders. Crocs' ability to build additional shoes within the season enabled it to take advantage of strong customer demand, resulting in the company filling in-season orders totaling many times that of the initial prebooked orders. The case describes the Crocs' supply chain. It asks students to assess the company's core competencies and how those can be exploited in the future. The case was revised in March 2011 to present information on the company's results in 2007 and prepare students for discussions of problems that would be faced in 2008 (covered in the B and C cases)."

Link to Module 4: This case is a great example of the essence of a dynamic capability and core competencies by having highly flexible competencies in sourcing, manufacturing, and distribution.

Wal-Mart, 2007

David B. Yoffie; Michael Slind
Product Number: 707517-PDF-ENG
Publication Date: March 01, 2007
Length: 12 pages

Description:

"In 2007, Wal-Mart faced challenges to its historically high growth rate. Lagging same-store sales and setbacks overseas led the company to consider strategic shifts. Wal-Mart was the world's largest retailer, but competition had become particularly acute as the company expanded from rural markets, which it had long dominated, into urban and suburban areas. Covers developments in Wal-Mart's merchandising strategy and its approach to store formats; its sometimes controversial human resources practices; its efforts to improve its image through a public relations campaign; its aggressive, though occasionally problematic, move into international markets; and its leading competitors, especially Target. Exhibits provide data (current as of February 2007) on Wal-Mart's financial performance, its stock-price performance, its international operations, and its store formats, as well as on Target's financial performance."

Link to Module 4: This case shows that before considering a strategic shift, a company needs to assess the resources, dynamic capabilities, and competencies of its business model.

Below is a recommended Harvard Business Publishing article available for purchase at www.hbsp.harvard.edu

Competing on Resources

David J. Collis; Cynthia A. Montgomery
Product Number: R0807N-PDF-ENG
Publication Date: July 01, 2008
Length: 12 pages

Description:

"This article was originally published in July–August 1995 and was republished in July–August 2008 as an HBR Classic. This article includes a one-page preview that quickly summarizes the key ideas and provides an overview of how the concepts work in practice along with suggestions for further reading. How do you create and sustain a profitable strategy? Many approaches have focused managers' attention inward, urging them to build a unique set of corporate resources and capabilities. In practice, however, identifying and developing core competence too often becomes a feel-good exercise that no one fails. Collis and Montgomery, of Harvard Business School, explain how a company's resources drive its performance in a dynamic competitive environment, and they offer a framework that moves strategic thinking forward in two ways. The resource-based view of the firm comprises a pragmatic and rigorous set of market tests to determine whether a company's resources are truly valuable enough to serve as the basis for strategy and integrates that market view with earlier insights about competition and industry structure. Where a company chooses to play will determine its profitability as much as its resources do. The authors spell out in clear managerial terms why some competitors are more profitable than others, how to put the idea of core competence into practice, and how to develop diversification strategies that make sense. To illustrate the power of resource-based strategies, the authors provide many examples of organizations—including Disney, Cooper, Sharp, and Newell—that have been able to use corporate resources to establish and maintain competitive advantage at the business-unit level and also to benefit from the attractiveness of the markets in which they compete."

Link to Module 4: This article discusses how companies use strategically valuable resources to perform activities better than rivals to achieve a competitive advantage.

Note: Descriptions are from www.hbsp.harvard.edu with permission.

Recommended McKinsey & Company article available free at
www.mckinseyquarterly.com

Building Organizational Capabilities

McKinsey Global Survey Results
Publication Date: January, 2010
Length: 7 pages

Description:

"Building organizational capabilities, such as leadership development or
lean operations, is a top priority for most companies. However, many of
them have not yet figured out how to do so effectively. The odds improve
at companies where senior leaders are more involved."

Direct link to article: http://www.mckinseyquarterly.com/Building
_organizational_capabilities_McKinsey_Global_Survey_results_2540

Link to Module 4: This survey shows that when executives set the capabilities agenda as a priority, their company is more effective at building
the capabilities most important to performance.

Reflect on what you originally included on the first page of this module and how your understanding of the capabilities and competencies of your business model has changed. Are you ready to rethink your competitive advantage and take action?

MODULE 5

Business Model and Strategy

Building on the circle for competitive advantage and the triangle for business model, we use those shapes to light up the various strategies that make your business model successful.

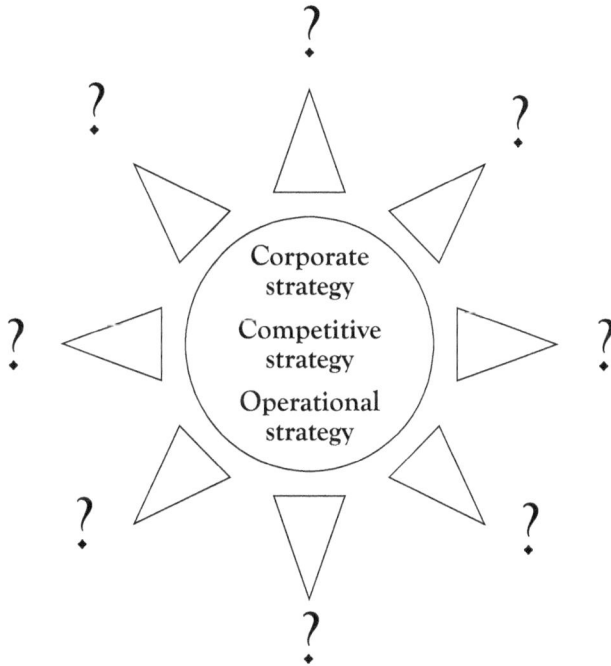

There are many types of growth strategies. In your view, what growth strategies exist to execute a business model? Use the triangles above to identify strategies used by organizations before going to the next page.

Imagine an orange sun to project the strategies in the market place

Objectives

1. Understand the concept of strategy.
2. Use real-world examples of companies' strategies.
3. Discuss strategic choices.

Prelude

Ask new questions and you can change the world! Changing the world in a strategy context is to create value by changing the rules of the game. Think of how Apple changed the world by changing the rules of the game with the PC, the iPhone, and the iPad. Apple did it with new products, new standards, and new strategies. When companies outline their strategies to effectively compete, they are using their ability to reduce market complexities to essential elements by rethinking value for the consumer, restructuring processes, and often reinventing their business model. In the book *The Laws of Simplicity*, John Maeda, a world-renowned graphic designer, a professor at MIT and President of the Rhode Island School of Design, explains that the first law of simplicity is "reduce." For example, he sites that technology features should not be added just because we can add them. Instead his guide to simplicity in the digital age is a continuous flow of questions which leads to his last (tenth) law called "The One" where he tells us that "simplicity is about subtracting the obvious, and adding the meaningful."[1] His book is relevant and inspiring for this context because the goal of corporate strategy is to create value. What is meaningful to an organization can indeed be developed into a value creating and capturing process, the essence of strategy.

Strategies have been defined as a plan of action. It is a concept that is concrete yet abstract. Looking at strategy from a business model perspective makes it more concrete because it stipulates that your business model is the basis to deliver your strategies. Strategies are mechanisms of action to deliver and capture the value created in a business model. (A mechanism of action is a term used in Pharmacology which refers to the specific biochemical interaction through which a substance produces its effect.) It is about showing what you are good at. Strategy is a set of actions that a company takes given its strategic and financial goals, capabilities and competencies, and performance objectives to achieve a competitive advantage reflected in a profitable business model. This module presents three levels of strategies with a business model approach to growth in an organization. At the corporate level, companies make strategic choices with a view for long-term performance. At the competitive level, also called business level, the focus is on competing with differentiation or low cost. At the operational level, also called functional level, efficiencies and dynamic processes drive the value.

Characteristics of a Sound Strategy

A sound strategy fits external opportunities to internal capabilities, builds a sustainable competitive advantage, and achieves both strategic and financial goals. Companies develop strategies that align opportunities to their business model by using their capabilities and competencies to execute strategies that will build a competitive advantage and improve company performance. The speed with which a strategy can be implemented is critical and a function of the business model. Building on previous modules, the following characteristics are applied to the levels of strategy which are later discussed in this module.

Characteristics of strategy	Levels of strategy
Aligns opportunity to strategic and financial goals	Corporate level
Uses capabilities and competencies for competitive advantage	Competitive level
Achieves performance objectives with financial and operational metrics	Operational level

Strategy

What is strategy? It is the fuel for your business model. Recall the analogy in Module 2: the business model is the engine and the strategic direction is the fuel. Developing strategies is one of the four components of setting a strategic direction. Your strategies are the choices you make regarding whether or not you have the operations to pursue a market opportunity. If there is a good fit between your business model capabilities and the opportunity, your strategies at the corporate, competitive, and operational levels will determine your success. As shown in Figure 1, there are three levels of strategies: corporate, competitive (also called business level), and operational (also called functional level). Strategic choices in each area impact the other areas. For example, a corporate strategy of horizontal integration where one competitor acquires another competitor will result in operational changes due to redundancies and create new competitive and operational strategies. Your strategies complement your business model which helps decide which strategic option is best for a company. One academic study also states that both competitive advantage and performance are enhanced when business models and strategies are complements (see Appendix B).

Strategies and Business Model Performance

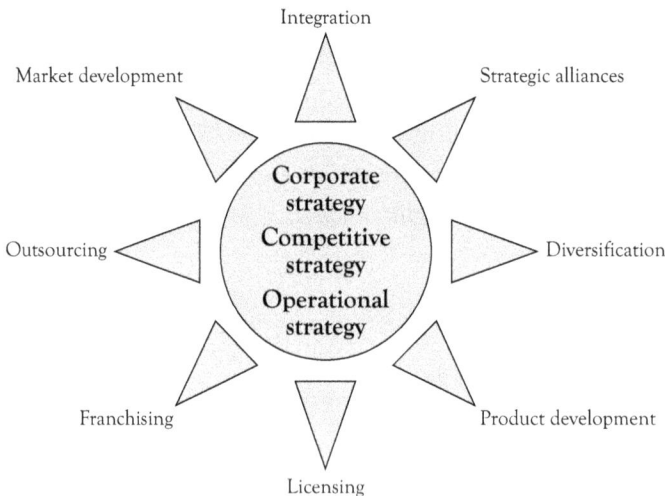

Figure 5. Components of strategy.

The relationship between your business model and your strategies is in understanding your business model to choose and implement strategies. This in turn is based on your capacity to identify the strategic resources with which to build dynamic processes resulting in the right competencies to deliver the value proposition. The test of a strategy is how well a company uses its business model capabilities and competencies to deliver profitable results (business model performance).

Strategy Versus Operations

You use your operations to carry out your strategies. Your strategies are developed as a result of having certain dynamic capabilities. Your strategies are only as good as what your operations can deliver. It was recently reported in the *Wall Street Journal* that 65% of companies in the Standard & Poors 500-stock index point to strategic and operational errors as the main cause of poor results of companies who missed their earnings target for the first quarter of 2012. The study conducted by ValueBridge Advisors specified that strategic risks involved the business environment and the companies' business models. Operational risks were defined as processes, systems, or human resources (HR) issues and were the primary cause of poor results. Inevitably, "if you screw up your strategic decision, you're going to stress your operations."[2]

Strategy Development

The traditional process of formulating strategy is to identify the threats and opportunities in your environment, utilize your strengths to take advantage of opportunities, minimize the threats, and develop a competitive advantage. According to a McKinsey study, the key is to have a dedicated corporate development process integrated with other management processes such as operating reviews, budgeting, and talent development. The study reveals that multibusiness companies that have a consistent corporate strategy development process achieve greater profitability because they are forced to think about reallocating resources among business units. The process includes addressing corporate-level strategy questions on a planning cycle to review specific inputs such as industry dynamics, company performance, competitor strategies, financial projections, and operational benchmarking.[3] Strategy developed from a business model framework is a more integrated approach to achieve a good fit between your capabilities, competencies, and strategies which mitigates the risk of choosing the wrong strategy.

Corporate Strategy

Corporate strategies to grow revenues and earnings over time follow a growth strategy continuum. Companies grow from a single business to multiple business units by making strategy choices which include intensive growth, integration, diversification, and restructuring.

For a single business to grow its revenues and earnings, the strategies are market development (sell existing products to new markets), product development (sell new products to existing markets), and market penetration (sell more of what you make). Pursuing intensive growth strategies allows a company to leverage competencies. The next strategy choices on the continuum are growth through integration strategies such as backward integration (upstream), forward integration (downstream), and horizontal integration (buy competitors and grow market share). Pursuing integration strategies allows a company to achieve economies of scale and yield a competitive advantage. The next growth strategies on the continuum are diversification strategies. A company diversifies internally or externally by acquisition, merger, or joint venture. The diversification can be related or unrelated to the current business. Related diversification can result in cost sharing, skills and competency transfer, and greater strategic fit (operational fit, management fit, marketing fit). Unrelated diversification is more an investment decision for portfolio restructuring and financial economies (efficient internal capital market, restructuring assets). Pursuing diversification strategies allows a company to achieve economies of scope and improve financial performance. Google's new focus on hardware is a shift from its revenue-driven strategy of selling advertising to a related diversification strategy in order to protect its core search business, achieve economies of scope and improve their financial performance.[4]

In addition, as companies diversify, they may also divest some of their existing business units to reconfigure their portfolio and reallocate resources for better returns or they may have to turn around their operations. Restructuring choices include turnaround, retrenchment, divestment, liquidation, and bankruptcy. Companies need to restructure when the costs of operations are too high, the performance objectives cannot be met, and the strategies are not working. Restructuring often includes a change in leadership to reassess or change the business model, reset the strategic direction, and divest of nonstrategic assets in order to improve the profitability of remaining operations. Restructuring may also include making acquisitions to build dynamic capabilities and competencies to better compete with a business strategy of low-cost or differentiation supported by the appropriate operational strategies.

Corporate-level strategies address where to allocate your resources. A business model requires strategic resources to build capabilities and competencies. As such, corporate strategy maintains the sustainability of a business model.

Competitive Strategy

The purpose of a competitive strategy is to gain a competitive advantage. One way of measuring a competitive advantage is to compare operating profit margins to those of the competitive space participants as well as to industry averages. Those results are based on the capabilities and competencies of an organization's business model which ultimately determine its ability to compete. The pursuit of a low-cost strategy and a differentiation strategy require different resources and capabilities as discussed above.

From a business model perspective, competitive strategies are primarily revenue-driven strategies but also include cost-driven strategies. When business models are discussed by analysts on the financial networks, the competitiveness of a company often centers on its revenue streams and its cost structure as a way to compete.

Operational Strategy

Operational strategies are also called functional strategies in each of the functions or departments of a company. They include strategies in HR, marketing, manufacturing, research and development, finance, and social networking. Although companies are structured by departments, many companies operate as matrix organizations to remain flexible and adaptable. More and more cross-functional teams play a critical role in capability building for effective strategy execution. For example, as you reconfigure teams to solve problems or develop new products, or both, you are using an operational strategy to have greater impact on the success of your competitive strategy (differentiation or low cost). As a result, one HR operational strategy would be to train employees in project management skills including how to perform in cross-functional product development teams. This in turn would develop a dynamic capability given the new mix of strategic resources used for new product development.

From a business model perspective, operational strategies are primarily cost-driven strategies but also include revenue-driven strategies. The sources of cost competitiveness and differentiation are in the capabilities, competencies, and dynamic processes integral to the business model.

Building and Restructuring the Business Model-Centric Organization

Corporate strategies on a growth continuum go through the corporate strategy choices of intensive growth, integration, and diversification. Concomitantly, organizations that have made acquisitions or merged with others or have grown to a point of diseconomies of scale and scope need to restructure. The idea is to continuously seek ways to achieve a portfolio of businesses and competencies that will enhance your business model in terms of other revenue streams, efficient cost structure, better value proposition, embedded capabilities and competencies, and greater profitability. Earnings can be managed by offsetting restructuring charges in some businesses with improvements in others.

Strategies are developed by companies to achieve a competitive advantage in an industry but more importantly it is to redefine and create new industries. Apple and CNN achieved precisely that! How did they do it? What did it take to think this way? It started with a new value proposition, an understanding of what it would take in terms of capabilities, the revenue possibilities, and cost implications. Once they understood their business model, they concentrated on product development and market development strategies to compete with existing dominant companies like IBM, NBC, CBS and ABC. They then followed a growth pattern as well as a restructuring pattern.

Business Model and Strategy Applications

To interactively learn the relationship between a business model and strategy, below are

1. Three interactive "Enter the Boardroom" applications to learn the three levels of strategy as they relate to the key components of a business model.
2. One exercise to develop your strategy skills from a business model perspective.

1. Enter the Boardroom Interactive Applications

The "Enter the Boardroom" series consist of brief stories of companies to illustrate key concepts in each module. Imagine that you are an independent board member questioning decisions made by applying the concepts you learned. To be in an interactive learning environment, read each company scenario below with the corresponding concept and reflect on who should be at the table, what the agenda should consist of, and what the outcome(s) might be. This will also give you some thoughts for your own questions.

Enter the Boardroom Series: Strategy

Yum Brands, Kellogg, Amazon

What Is a Corporate Strategy? The Yum Story[5]

A corporate level strategy answers two basic questions on a continuing basis: What business(es) should we be in? and Where should we allocate our resources? in order to add value and long-term profitability. A corporate strategy starts with a commitment at the corporate level to allocate resources to the business(es) that are most promising. The answers to those questions come from the leadership. Senior management is responsible for continuous strategic reviews of the performance of their businesses, their global markets, and their growth potential; the board of directors is responsible to further question the corporate strategy choices of senior management.

Corporate strategies include growth or retrenchment in global markets (national and international markets). Growth strategies include market penetration, market development, product development, vertical integration, diversification, strategic alliances, licensing, and franchising. Retrenchment strategies include turnaround, divestment, liquidation, and bankruptcy.

One example is Yum Brands Inc. which owns KFC, Taco Bell, and Pizza Hut. They describe their growth plans in the businesses they are

(Continued)

in and how they will allocate their resources. Given a review of the performance of their brands, they are allocating resources to reinvent the Taco for international markets and reposition the KFC brand in the United States. They have corporate-owned stores in the fastest growing markets and are cutting their exposure to the saturated US market with franchising.[6] (For more information on the Yum story, read the article cited in the notes and references starting on p. 157.)

Enter the Yum Boardroom

Who should be in the boardroom?
What is the agenda?
Why?

You are now a board member of Yum. Be prepared to answer the following questions:

1. What markets have the most growth potential?
2. Why is the US market not performing as well?
3. How is your franchising strategy working?

(Continued)

Prepare your own questions for the other members of the board:

4. What …
5. Why …
6. How …
7. Other questions.

What Is a Competitive Strategy? The Kellogg Story[7]

A competitive strategy answers one basic question: how to compete based on our competencies. Companies have two strategic choices: to compete on low cost, which means that the company's cost structure allows for lower prices while achieving good margins, or to compete on differentiation, which means that the company's products are unique, fulfill a gap in customer needs, and prices can be set higher. Therefore, to add value from their business units, companies need to perform activities at lower costs, perform activities in a differentiated way for which they can charge premium prices, and have competencies at the business unit level. Companies can also pursue an integrated cost-leadership and differentiation strategy.

What competencies are needed to support a successful competitive strategy?

- *Cost leadership:* Manufacturing and materials management
- *Differentiation:* Research & development, sales, marketing

(Both can be pursued targeting a broad or a narrow market niche)

Kellogg started out as a cereal company. They have had slow overall growth. They have become a three-business unit company: cereal, snacks, and frozen and specialty foods. They recently made the acquisition of Pringles from Procter & Gamble for $2.7 billion. Although the acquisition is a corporate level strategy, we will view it from the business level regarding Kellogg's ability to compete better.[8] (For more information on Kellogg, read the article cited in the notes and references starting on p. 157.)

(*Continued*)

Enter the Kellogg Boardroom

Who should be in the boardroom?
What is the agenda?
Why?

You are now a board member of Kellogg. Be prepared to answer the following questions:

1. What competencies does Pringles have to make snacks a successful business?
2. Why is Kellogg developing their snack business?
3. How is Kellogg competing: low cost or differentiation?

Prepare your own questions for the other members of the board:

4. What ...
5. Why ...
6. How ...
7. Other questions.

(Continued)

What Is an Operational Strategy? The Amazon Story[9]

The rubber hits the road at the operational level. It is where your operational strategies in marketing, finance, logistics, and operations provide the necessary support to carry out your competitive strategy of low cost or differentiation. An operational strategy is also known as a functional strategy because it refers to the various functions or departments of an organization. As companies realize the importance of integrated operations, an operational strategy is more reflective of the business model and the need to cut across the silos of functional areas in order to develop competencies that are hard to copy.

A good example of a company that epitomizes the importance of operations is Amazon. Amazon evolved from retailing books on the Internet to retailing everything on the Internet. They invested heavily in state-of-the-art warehousing and distribution facilities when no one else was investing. They were adding to their competency in order to increase their efficiency with lower costs of inputs, economies of scale, and innovation. They are now in the reading devices and tablet computer business with Kindle Fire as a new revenue stream. What you do at the operational level affects your sales but, most importantly, your operating margins. Here is the situation at Amazon:

- Fourth quarter 2011 revenue rose by 35%
- Profits decreased by 57%
- Operating expenses rose by 38%
- 67% Increase in workforce from 2010

Amazon continues to spend heavily on warehouse logistics and operations, technology, and Kindle, but the revenue growth is not keeping pace and profits are lower.[10] (For more information on Amazon, read the article cited in the notes and references starting on p. 157.)

(Continued)

Enter the Amazon Boardroom

Who should be in the boardroom?
What is the agenda?
Why?

Be prepared to answer the following questions and to ask your own "what, why, and how" questions to the board members:

1. What are Amazon's operational strategies?
2. Why are Amazon's operating margins declining?
3. How is Amazon's low-cost strategy working?

Prepare your own questions for the other members of the board:

4. What …
5. Why …
6. How …
7. Other questions.

2. Strategy Analysis

We have talked about how to view an organization in terms of its alignment of capabilities and competencies to strategy in order to carry out its business model. The example that we will use for this analysis is The Dollar Shave Club. It is an e-commerce start-up that sells razor blades for a $3–$9 monthly fee—the subscription model. The idea is "shaking things up" in the razor market for companies like Procter & Gamble's Gillette business unit.[11]

- The sale of razor blades has not shown any volume increase in the past 40–50 years.
- The price of razors blades bought through traditional retailers like drugstores is too expensive.
- Competitors are already launching other e-commerce subscription models.
- The Dollar Shave Club identified the "pain point" in buying razors blades—it cost too much—a key consumer need to have affordable razor blades.
- The Dollar Shave Club developed the need into a business model.

Strategy Analysis Exercise

1. Now you are charged with developing strategies for The Dollar Shave Club that will give them a competitive advantage.

   - What are/should be their corporate, competitive, and operational strategies?
   - What are they doing differently?
   - Is it sustainable?

2. Identify capability and competency areas of the Dollar Shave Club.
3. Identify appropriate strategies that align to those areas.
4. Based on your analysis, answer the questions above.
5. Present recommendations as an analyst.

Guidance for the Manager:

Key Points on Strategy

- The risk of choosing the wrong strategies is mitigated when your business model is clearly defined.
- Your strategies are only as good as how well you understand your business model.
- Strategies are dependent on your company's capacity to change.
- From a business model perspective, strategies help to minimize costs and maximize revenues.
- Strategies based on a sound business model increase the capacity for competitive advantage.

Add your own key points:

Below is a recommended Harvard Business Publishing case available for purchase at www.hbsp.harvard.edu

HUGE and Digital Strategy

Ramon Casadesus-Masanell; Nicholas G. Karvounis
Product number: 712442-PDF-ENG
Revision Date: January 09, 2011
Publication Date: October 28, 2011
Length: 22 pages

Description:

"In 2011, HUGE, Inc. is the fastest growing digital agency in the United States. Its CEO, Aaron Shapiro, is considering a set of novel growth strategies to take his firm to the next level. However, the digital strategy industry in which HUGE has made a name for itself is highly fluid and constantly evolving—the options facing Shapiro and HUGE must be considered in light of an industry structure that blurs the lines across competitors, complements, and clients and could easily shift for or against digital agencies such as HUGE in the near future. Using HUGE as a focal point, students are asked to evaluate competitive dynamics in the digital strategy industry and predict the evolution of the market. They are also asked to use the unique dynamics of the digital strategy industry as a backdrop for assessing HUGE's best growth option going forward."

Link to Module 5: This case expands growth strategy choices for a company to improve its business model performance.

Below are recommended Harvard Business Publishing articles available for purchase at www.hbsp.harvard.edu

Building a Business Model and Strategy: How They Work Together

Product Number: 5337BC-PDF-ENG
Publication Date: Oct 30, 2004
Harvard Business Press Chapters
Length: 20 pages
Harvard Business Essentials: Entrepreneur's Toolkit

Description:

"As this chapter explains, a business model identifies your customers and describes how your business will profitably address their needs. Strategy, on the other hand, is about how to differentiate your business and give it competitive advantage. Using sample cases and step-by-step instructions, this chapter reiterates that both are required for success and explains how to develop them."

Link to Module 5: This chapter further explains the difference between a business model and a strategy and how a business model drives a strategy.

How to Make the Most of Your Company's Strategy

Stephen Bungay
Product Number: R1101L-PDF-ENG
Publication Date: January 01, 2011
Length: 10 pages

Description:

"Corporate strategy often seems abstract to managers on the ground, who struggle to translate it into a realistic plan of action. But a process called strategy briefing, which originated with the military, can help them overcome that challenge. Bungay, the director of the Ashridge Strategic Management Centre, describes in this article how briefings can move managers and their reports from confusion about a complex set of goals and performance measures to clarity about just which objectives each person needs to focus on and in what order. Using a fictional case study as an illustration, Bungay outlines the five critical steps of the process: (1) state your intent, or what you are expected to do and why, (2) revise it in the context of your company's situation, (3) determine which measures indicate whether you're achieving your goal, (4) define the tasks implied by your intent, and (5) define the boundaries, or constraints, that limit your team. A single strategy briefing can help a team perform better, but the real magic happens when briefings roll down through an entire organization. When that occurs, the company's strategy is broken into a cascade of discrete but linked elements. In the end, people will be strategically aligned and operationally autonomous—a combination that is one of the hallmarks of high-performance organizations."

Link to Module 5: This article explains how to define what a strategy is.

How to Best Divest

Michael C. Mankins; David Harding; Rolf-Magnus Weddigen
Product Number: R0810F-PDF-ENG
Publication Date: October 01, 2008
Length: 10 pages

Description:

"This article includes a one-page preview that quickly summarizes the key ideas and provides an overview of how the concepts work in practice along with suggestions for further reading. Most corporations are not as skilled at selling off assets as they are at buying them, often divesting at the wrong time or in the wrong way. Either is a very expensive mistake. A Bain & Company study has found that over the last 20 years, corporations that took a disciplined approach to divestiture created nearly twice as much value for shareholders as the average firm. In this article, Bain partners Mankins, Harding, and Weddigen set out the four straightforward rules those effective divestors follow. First: Just as they have acquisition teams, smart divestors have full-time divestiture groups, which continually screen their companies' portfolios for likely businesses to sell off and think through the timing and implementation steps needed to maximize value in each particular case. Second: They choose their divestiture candidates objectively. Too many firms rush to sell in economic downturns, when prices are low. Thoughtful divestors will sell only those businesses that do not fit with the corporation's core and are not worth more to themselves than they are to any other company. Third: Successful divestors consider how to structure a deal and to whom they will sell as carefully as they consider what units to sell and when. And they are as meticulous about planning the implementation of a deal as savvy acquirers are about postmerger integration. Fourth: They make a compelling case for how, and how quickly, the deal will benefit the buyer, and they make sure the selling unit's employees will be motivated to stay on and realize that value. Using these four rules, companies as diverse as Textron, Weyerhaeuser, Ford, Groupe Danone, and Roche have become "divesture ready": consistently able to sell at the right time and in the right way to create the most value for their shareholders."

Link to Module 5: This article relates to restructuring and building an organization based on its business model.

Note: Descriptions are from www.hbsp.harvard.edu with permission.

Recommended McKinsey & Company articles available free at www.mckinseyquarterly.com

Managing the Strategy Journey

Chris Bradley; Lowell Bryan; Sven Smit
Publication Date: July, 2012
Strategy Practice

Description:

"Regular strategic dialogue involving a broad group of senior executives can help companies adapt to the unexpected. Here's one company's story, and some principles for everyone."

Direct link to article:
http://www.mckinseyquarterly.com/Managing_the_strategy_journey_2991

Link to Module 5: This article is an important story to create the right strategy that will support a business model.

Creating more value with corporate strategy

McKinsey Global Survey Results
Publication Date: January, 2011
Length: 4 pages

Description:

"Few companies create strategies that deliver more value than the sum of their business unit parts, but those that do also excel at moving resources and removing barriers."

Direct link to article:

http://www.mckinseyquarterly.com/Creating_more_value_with_corpo rate_strategy_McKinsey_Global_Survey_results_2733

Link to Module 5: This article examines the use of resources to develop a strategy and create more value.

Reflect on what you originally included on the first page of this module and how your understanding of the relationship between a business model and a strategy has changed. Are you ready to review your strategies and take action?

MODULE 6

Business Model and Innovation

Building on the triangle, we have chosen a star because companies that support innovation can become stars in their field.

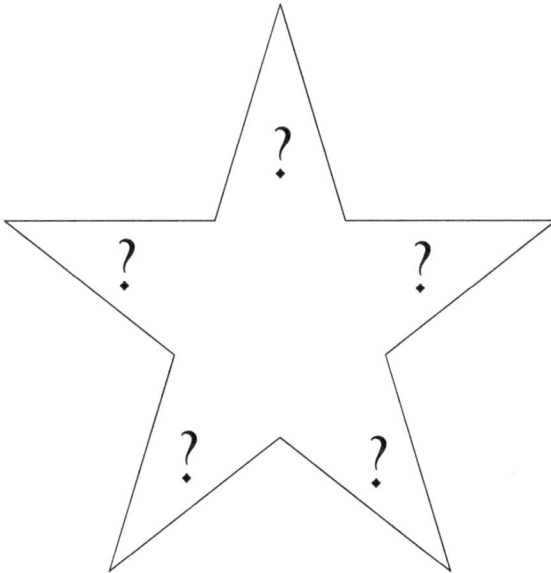

In your view, how can innovation improve a business model? Use the above star shape to identify five elements necessary to build a capacity to innovate in an organization before going to the next page.

Imagine a yellow star to activate creativity

Objectives

1. Understand the relationship between business model and innovation.
2. Use real-world examples of innovation in companies.
3. Discuss innovation choices.

Prelude

Leonardo da Vinci used the beauty of nature for the "attainment of creative power."[1] Using such perspectives is one way to bring about inspired and innovative thinking. Leonardo accepted the concept that the universe was "an all-inclusive sphere with four elements in concentric regions: earth occupied the center, surrounding it was water, then a layer of air, and enveloping the whole was fire."[2] He was interested in the configuration of these elements as the driving forces of the universe. Similarly, previous modules focused on the configuration of resources to build dynamic capabilities as drivers of business model performance. Innovation also means recombining capabilities by exploiting the dynamics of current capabilities. In this module, we are guided by Leonardo's courage in his time to innovate in our time. This module is about understanding innovation to create value that can be described as a work of art.

Innovation begins with inspiration. Inspiration is a muse. Listen to your muse and apply its spirit in what you are trying to create. Leonardo became an innovative artist because he found his muse through music, the arts, and the sciences. His notebooks reveal his passion and curiosity for all branches of knowledge.

Inspiration is pervasive in all aspects of creating, developing, and managing a business model. In Module 1, the value proposition is a tribute to having been inspired. In Module 2, insight into metrics is a form of inspiration. In Module 3, crafting a vision is to inspire others. In Module 4, developing unique competencies requires inspiration. In Module 5, making strategic choices is a deep process of inspiration. In this module, innovation is defined as the capacity of an organization to keep its business model relevant and sustainable. As such, it focuses on the flow of an idea across the organization to provide solutions to emerging problems in the business model. For example, take a distribution problem and turn it into an innovation that positively impacts costs and revenues.

Characteristics of Sound Innovation

Innovation is to be inventive. To be inventive, organizations have rigorous innovation capabilities for process innovation and product innovation; they conduct innovation experiments, develop innovation strategies, and nurture innovation teams. An example is Anheuser-Busch's (AB) robust innovation process as described by Patrick O'Riordan, global director of innovation. They have a clear and robust innovation process that breaks down innovation into a front-end process involving consumer discovery work, idea formulation, and idea qualification, and a back-end process which is more rigid, having fixed stage gates, than the iterative front-end.[3] AB has two basic innovation strategies: "renovations" for "strengthening existing product lines" with new marketing campaigns and product improvements, and "innovations" for completely new products.[4] To have an innovation is to introduce something new: a new idea, method or device. From a business model perspective, it is an activity or a process that can be done differently or even eliminated to improve the revenues and cost structure. Ideally, it is a new configuration of how to fulfill a customer need that creates a revenue stream.

Innovation is a way to support a company's ability to compete and a critical element in the successful implementation of strategy. For example, we saw in Module 5 that companies have two basic choices of competitive strategies: differentiation and cost. A differentiation strategy requires product innovation to be sustainable. A cost-leadership strategy requires process innovation to be sustainable. A company that utilizes existing capabilities and competencies to exploit innovation in their business model develop compet-

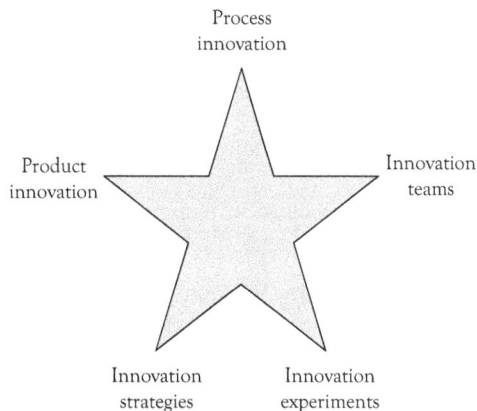

Figure 6. Components of Innovation.

itive advantages. For example, Gillette invests heavily in both product and process innovation. Its product innovation results in bringing a significant number of new products to the market every year which in turn, help sustain revenue growth. Its process innovation improves its design capabilities to produce products at lower costs which then add to its competitive advantage.

The relationship between a business model and innovation is that the capacity to innovate in all aspects of the business model is essential to a sustainable business model. Research conducted over the last 10 years further indicates the need for organizations to build a competency in business model innovation.[5] In this module, we focus on innovation to create value with an existing business model which may lead to entirely new business models.

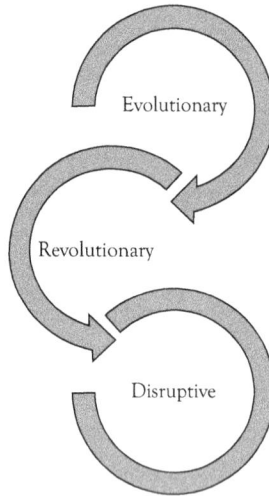

Figure 7. Types of Innovation.

The mode of innovation is a function of the solution, the market, and the innovative capacity of the business model. If the innovation is evolutionary it provides an expected solution to an existing market. If the innovation is revolutionary it provides a radical solution to a new market. If the innovation is disruptive it provides an unexpected solution to an existing market that had unserved customer needs. Organizations should approach innovation to achieve innovative solutions that are radical, expected, or unexpected by aiming for all the three types. In the case of disruptive innovation, Clayton M. Christensen replaced the term disruptive technology with disruptive innovation because the technology is not disruptive rather it enables the business model to create the disruptive impact in the industry.[6]

Drivers of Innovation

In Module 2 we discussed drivers of revenues, costs, and profits assuming the production and sale of current products and services. In Module 5 we talked about asking questions to strategize on the best choice. In this module, we are focused on nonexistent products and services, and asking unrelated questions. According to a study of 3,000 executives over a six-year period by Professors Clayton M. Christensen, Jeffrey Dyer. and Hal Gregersen, the drivers of innovation consist of five important discovery skills: associating, questioning, observing, experimenting, and networking. The most powerful driver was making connections across unrelated questions, problems, and ideas (associating). Using the power of association in the unified context of a business model can create evolutionary, revolutionary, and disruptive innovations capable of creating significant value. One technique used by McKinsey & Company to brainstorm new business model possibilities was to make connections between two unrelated companies. For example, comparing how Apple would design another company's retail stores. This helped executives think differently about their operations. This is exactly where the flow of an idea can begin ...

How to Innovate ... the Flow of an Idea

Let's continue with the example cited above where you now have a great idea for your retail stores. You know it will make a big difference in the operations, the performance, and the brand. Next step, do an experiment on a trial basis. It will allow you to rethink consumer needs and generate yet more ideas ... the flow of an idea.

To innovate in order to create more value with your business model has to do with operations and people. Hopefully your culture of innovation attracts only people who are attracted to this type of flexible, adaptable, innovative environment as in the case of Google. So if your company's capacity to innovate is integral to its business model and attracts people who are willing to be creative, you simply need the right structure to be innovative: product or process teams, experiments, incentives, and rewards.

"The best creative thinking happens on a company's front lines. You just need to encourage it."[7]

To create a culture of innovation wrapped around your business model, you need to explain innovation as part of the strategic objectives for the future performance and well-being of the company, facilitate innovation teams with the capacity to do experiments, and develop innovation strategies focused on employees, product, and process.

Product innovation: The development of ideas for new products is imperative to sustain revenue growth.

Process innovation: The development of capabilities to improve the cost structure is critical to add value in a business model-centric organization.

Innovation experiments: Intuit D4D (Design for Delight) replaced long PowerPoint presentations with experiments to learn directly from customers. Apple's project purple experiment became the iPhone. The innovativeness of 3M is to allow its employees to spend 15% of their time exploring side projects. It also offers seed money in the form of grants to encourage innovation.[8] 3M is viewed as an innovative company yet it spends little on R&D. Experiments are the real pursuit of innovation distributed across the organization.

Innovation strategies: Booz & Company's research shows that companies with robust open innovation capabilities (cross-boundary collaboration) are seven times as effective as firms with weak capabilities in generating returns on their R&D project investment portfolio. Companies (e.g., Procter & Gamble) with open innovation strategies (building links between inside groups and outsiders such as customers, inventors, academics, and even competitors) maintain leadership in their industries.[9] To design an innovation strategy is to determine the type (evolutionary, revolutionary, or disruptive), the focus (product or process or both), and the fit to the strategic goals and innovation capabilities.

Innovation Teams: The greatest innovators are employees. Google is a perfect example of a company that carries this belief. It is built to innovate because of its project teams that create a company and employee mind-set for innovation with its small work units, lots of experimentation, vigorous peer feedback, and a mission to improve the world.

Business Model and Innovation Applications

To interactively learn the relationship between a business model and innovation, below are

1. Three interactive "Enter the Boardroom" applications to learn how innovation can affect the success of a business model.
2. One exercise to develop your understanding of innovation from a business model perspective.

1. Enter the Boardroom Interactive Applications

The "Enter the Boardroom" series consist of brief stories of companies to illustrate key concepts in each module. Imagine that you are an independent board member questioning decisions made by applying the concepts you learned. To be in an interactive learning environment, read each company scenario below with the corresponding concept and reflect on who should be at the table, what the agenda should consist of, and what the outcome(s) might be. This will also give you some thoughts for your own questions.

Enter the Boardroom Series: Innovation

RIM, Zynga, Hewlett-Packard

What Is a Process Innovation? The Research in Motion Story[10]

A process innovation is a change in the way a product or service is manufactured, created, or distributed to achieve greater efficiencies. Process innovations are critical to the cost structure of a business model. When innovation occurs in a process, companies have to change the current process and as such must develop a capacity to change. In this case, change and innovation go hand in hand from making change happen to managing change which all adds up to developing a greater capacity to innovate.

Research in Motion (RIM) once a leading contender in the smartphone business for the corporate customer is now struggling to survive with its old phone technology in a highly competitive market. It appears that Blackberry, once was the envy of competitors, has been turned upside down with no upside in sight. Delay after delay have been announced for the new blackberry 10 phone and platform for apps.

(Continued)

RIM has a long history of missing deadlines as well as releasing products before they are fully finished.[11] This indicates a serious lack of process innovation to facilitate the manufacturing and sale of the new phones on time. One reason is that they are rebuilding their operating system from the ground up. Their saving grace is their revenue stream from Blackberry subscribers' access to its proprietary network. In the face of declining revenues, losses, and employee layoffs, "RIM is currently conducting a strategic review which includes everything from licensing the Blackberry 10 software to selling all or part of the company."[12] (For more information on the RIM story, read the article cited in the notes and references starting on p. 157.)

Enter the RIM Boardroom

Who should be in the boardroom?
What is the agenda?
Why?

You are now a board member of RIM. Be prepared to answer the following questions:

1. What can RIM do to improve its process innovation? Is it too late?
2. Why did RIM lose so much ground to competitors like Apple and Samsung?
3. How can RIM regain its capacity to innovate?

(Continued)

Prepare your own questions for the other members of the board:

4. What …
5. Why …
6. How …
7. Other questions.

What Is an Innovation Strategy? The Zynga Story[13]

An innovation strategy identifies the type of innovation that a company needs to pursue to sustain and strengthen its business model. A company needs to state its strategic intent regarding innovation and provide the necessary resources to encourage it. A company may be evolutionary or revolutionary in its drive to innovate given their business model and competitive space. An evolutionary innovation strategy can follow a product through its life-cycle extensions like Microsoft Windows Office versions. It can encompass a combination of key process areas that can significantly contribute to the profitability of the business model.

Sometimes it takes a market shift by competitors and product users to determine the viability of a business model. An innovation strategy can help a company create a market shift. In the case of Zynga, producing games is inherently an innovative business. The bigger innovation question, however, is how Zynga can sustain its business model given the shift to mobile. Zynga's executives defend the company's business model because they believe they have game-playing audiences interested in genres and styles which call for next generation sequels.[14] Does this point to an innovation strategy that was too narrow? (For more information on the Zynga story, read the article cited in the notes and references starting on p. 157.)

(Continued)

Enter the Zynga Boardroom

Who should be in the boardroom?
What is the agenda?
Why?

You are now a board member of Zynga. Be prepared to answer the following questions:

1. What is Zynga's innovation strategy?
2. Why is Zynga struggling in mobile games?
3. How can Zynga stay relevant?

Prepare your own questions for the other members of the board:

4. What ...
5. Why ...
6. How ...
7. Other questions.

What Is an Innovation Team? The HP story15

Building an innovation team requires a climate of innovation. An innovation team is a group of employees with the ability to provide unique solutions to drive product and process innovation.

(Continued)

HP began as the greatest story of a team of two engineers whose genetic DNA became the innovation DNA of Hewlett-Packard. HP Invent was the slogan. HP's growth came primarily from product innovation. As hardware, software, and services became more interdependent, acquisitions (such as EDS) became the vehicle for growth. HP's services business (17.5 billion) is the second biggest revenue generator behind computers (18.3 billion). Now HP is in a turnaround mode for the next few years with cost cutting and restructuring, layoffs of 8% (27,000) of their workforce, continued integration of acquisitions, and reorganization. Industry trends are working against the EDS model of outsourcing requiring large long-term contracts which are declining. Today HP is focusing its innovation on products and services for cost leadership.

"HP Labs actively seeks, develops, and performs research projects and programs in a range of future-facing technology areas that align with HP's strategic vision and goals. Our world-class staff of research scientists and engineers operates in cutting-edge facilities at seven locations around the world."[16,17] (For more information on HP, read the article cited in the notes and references starting on p. 157.)

Enter the HP Boardroom

Who should be in the boardroom?
What is the agenda?
Why?

(Continued)

You are now a board member of HP. Be prepared to answer the following questions:

1. What is HP's notion of innovation? Is it different than what it used to be?
2. Why did HP fall behind?
3. How is innovation impacting HP's performance?

Prepare your own questions for the other members of the board:

4. What ...
5. Why ...
6. How ...
7. Other questions.

2. Innovation Analysis

We have discussed the significance of innovation to a sound business model and different ways an organization can become more inventive. The example we will use in this innovation analysis is Groupon.

- Groupon's main value proposition is to offer consumers daily deals on local businesses.
- Groupon's CEO Andrew Mason describes the strategy as making Groupon the "operating system for local commerce."[18]
- At the same time, the company's executives state that its international operations, which make up more than half of its revenues, need a technology upgrade and other upkeep.[19]
- Groupon is also having problem recruiting an adequate and quality sale force.[20]

Innovation Analysis Exercise

1. Look into Groupon's 10 K to understand its recent performance, vision, mission, strategies, and future plans.
2. Identify three key areas that Groupon should immediately focus its innovation efforts on.
3. Suggest one innovation strategy (use the star figure as a guide) for each of those areas that need immediate innovation.
4. Identify new possible competencies/capabilities that Groupon needs to develop to successfully carry out the above suggested innovation strategies.
5. Discuss how such innovation will impact Groupon's business model.
6. Present recommendations as an analyst.

Guidance for the Manager:

Key Points on Innovation

- A company's capacity to innovate will keep the business model relevant.
- The most powerful driver of innovation is to make connections from unrelated questions, problems, and ideas across the organization.
- A culture of innovation allows a company to create more value with its business model.
- Innovation experiments create the conditions that support a climate of internal innovation.
- Innovation strategies determine the innovation agenda in a business model-centric organization.

Add your own key points:

Below are recommended Harvard Business Publishing cases available for purchase at: www.hbsp.harvard.edu

Applied Research Technologies, Inc.: Global Innovation's Challenges

Christopher A. Bartlett; Heather Beckham

Product Number: 4168-PDF-ENG

Publication Date: February 19, 2010

Length: 11 pages

Description:

"Applied Research Technologies, Inc. (ART) is a diversified technology company which has used its entrepreneurial culture and encouragement of innovation as an ongoing competitive advantage. The case concentrates on the challenges faced by Peter Vyas, the Filtration Unit manager, who must decide whether to request $2 million in project funding from the divisional vice president, Cynthia Jackson. Similar Filtration projects have failed twice before, damaging the credibility of the Filtration Unit and Vyas personally. Jackson has recently been challenged to turn around or shut down the unit. Students must determine a strategy from the perspectives of both a unit manager and a division VP. This two-tier focus provides the opportunity to analyze the management decision process at different levels of the organization. Topics include empowerment, project management, and managing innovation.

Topics Include: Managing Innovation, International Business, Organizational Behavior, Empowerment, Teams, Corporate Culture, Entrepreneurship, Project Management, Delegation, Corporate Strategy, and Diversified Technology."

Link to Module 6: This case provides a clear example of a culture of innovation.

If We Ran the World

Hanna Halaburda; Radka Dohnalova; Aldo Sesia

Product Number: 711490-PDF-ENG

Revision Date: Oct 28, 2011

Publication Date: March 16, 2011

Length: 15 pages

Description:

"Cindy Gallop launched IfWeRanTheWorld (IWRTW) in February 2010, as what the tech world called minimum viable product, in order to real-world test Gallop's "business of the future" concept while development was ongoing. IWRTW was conceived to bring together human good intentions with corporate good intentions, to activate both into shared action, against shared goals, to deliver shared and mutually accountable results. She wanted to make "doing good as sexy as hell" for both individuals and businesses, to make it quicker, easier, and simpler to turn intention into action, one "microaction" at a time. In January 2011, Gallop's key challenge was how to amplify the IWRTW experience in a way that would make it a more valuable-and immediately understandable-business proposition to a brand. The idea behind the venture was only as good as its business model and its execution."

Link to Module 6: This case offers insights into the development of a business model from the idea stage to the execution stage.

Below is a recommended Harvard Business Publishing simulation available for purchase at www.hbsp.harvard.edu

Strategic Innovation Simulation: Back Bay Battery (v2)

Clayton M. Christensen; Willy Shih

Product Number: 7015-HTM-ENG

Publication Date: Apr 05, 2012

Length: 90 min

Description:

"In this single-player simulation, students play the role of a business unit manager at a battery company facing the classic Innovator's Dilemma. Students have to manage R&D investment trade-offs between the unit's existing battery technology versus investing in a new, potentially disruptive battery technology. Over the course of eight simulated years, students must address a number of challenges including the timing and level of investment across both mature and new businesses, choices regarding market opportunities and inherent product performance characteristics, requirements to meet constraining financial objectives and constant trade-offs between investment options, all in the context of uncertain market information. The entire simulation can be played in 1.5 seat hours, plus debrief. This second release of the web-based Strategic Innovation Simulation: Back Bay Battery combines the proven learning objectives and storyline of the original with an updated user experience and enhanced administrative features. A Teaching Note contains an overview of theory, simulation screens, and reference materials. Pricing for corporate learning purchases is available. Please contact Customer Service."

Link to Module 6: This simulation gives students the opportunity to manage the trade-off between existing technology and disruptive technology.

Below is a recommended Harvard Business Publishing article available for purchase at www.hbsp.harvard.edu

When One Business Model Isn't Enough

Ramon Casadesus-Masanell; Jorge Tarzijan

Product Number: R1201M-PDF-ENG

Publication Date: January 01, 2012

Length: 6 pages

Description:

"Trying to operate two business models at once often causes strategic failure. Yet LAN Airlines, a Chilean carrier, runs three models successfully. Casadesus-Masanell, of Harvard Business School, and Tarzijan, of the Pontificia Universidad Catolica de Chile, explore how LAN has integrated a full-service international passenger model with a premium air-cargo business model while separately operating a no-frills passenger model for domestic flights. LAN's multimodel success comes from recognizing the complementarity of its two high-end services and the distinct, or substitute, nature of its no-frills offering. LAN came to that insight by analyzing the major assets that the models share and the compatibility of the models' operational resources and capabilities. It recognized that the more the models have in common, the more likely they are to generate greater value together than apart; the less they share, the more likely they are to be best executed separately. Nevertheless, managing multiple models is a tall order. LAN has had to face greater complexity, broaden its organizational skills, increase the flexibility of its workforce, and make other investments. But by mastering three models, the company has built formidable advantages that are difficult for competitors to overcome. Its example has shown how, properly applied, the implementation of multiple business models is not a risk but rather a new tool for strategists."

Link to Module 6: This article goes into the development of multiple business models as a way to mitigate risk and develop competitive advantages.

Note: Descriptions are from www.hbsp.harvard.edu with permission.

Recommended McKinsey & Company articles available free at www. mckinseyquarterly.com

Wiring the open-source enterprise

Jacques Bughin

Publication Date: January, 2012

McKinsey Global Institute

Description:

"Social technologies lie at the core of a new model that spurs user participation and speeds up product innovation."

Direct link to article:

http://www.mckinseyquarterly.com/Wiring_the_open-source_enterprise_2912

Link to Module 6: This article gives more insights into drivers of innovation.

Sparking creativity in teams: An executive's guide

Marla M. Capozzi; Renée Dye; Amy Howe

Publication Date: April, 2011

Strategy Practice

Description:

"Senior managers can apply practical insights from neuroscience to make themselves—and their teams—more creative."

Direct link to article:

http://www.mckinseyquarterly.com/Sparking_creativity_in_teams_An_executives_guide_2786

Link to Module 6: This article provides an example of the use of unrelated questions to drive innovation.

Recommended MIT Sloan article available free at: (www.sloanreview.mit.edu)

How to Identify New Business Models

Joseph V. Sinfield; Edward Calder;

Bernard McConnell; Steve Colson

Publication Date: December 21, 2011

Description:

"Systematically exploring alternative approaches to value creation can allow companies to find new opportunities for growth."

Direct link to article:

http://sloanreview.mit.edu/the-magazine/2012-winter/53214/how-to-identify-new-business-models

Link to Module 6: This article gives interesting clues to develop new business models.

Reflect on what you originally included on the first page of this module and how your understanding of innovation in a business model-centric organization has changed. Are you ready to create a culture of innovation and take action?

MODULE 7

Business Model Agenda

This module uses all the geometric shapes to show the collective agenda necessary to develop a business model-centric organization.

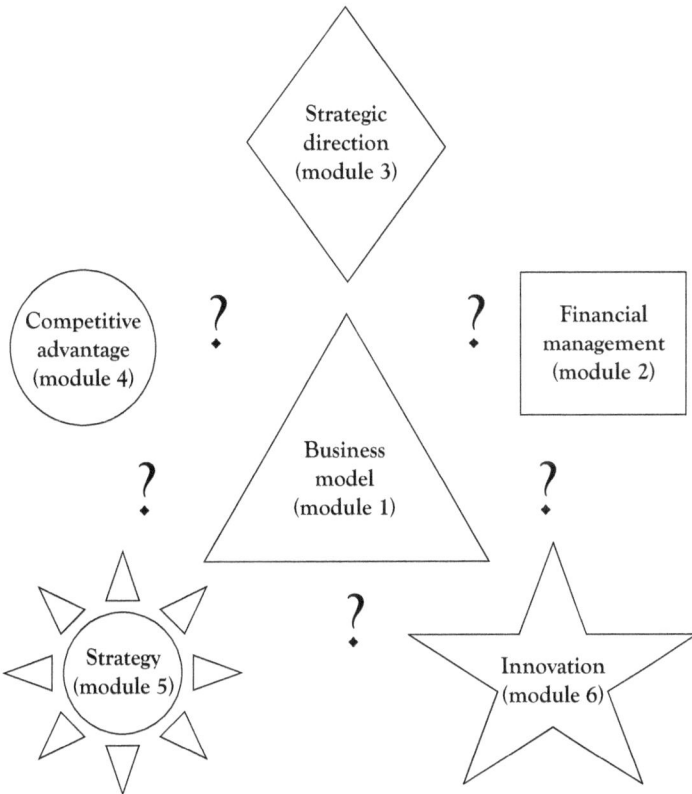

In your view, how do the various modules interrelate to build a business model-centric organization?

Objectives

1. Understand the concept of business model agenda.
2. Use business model value creation as a tool.
3. Develop a business model-centric mind-set creatively.

Prelude

Paris, 1982, an extraordinary experiment is conducted called the Aspect experiment. It includes a team of physicists who confirms quantum theory: that reality as we know does not exist at the subatomic level. It is reported in a book called *Beyond the Quantum*.[1] It is appropriate to make the leap from business to science for a moment for two reasons: it is inspiring and it's all about experiments. Although business is a reality, finding answers to the great metaphysical questions of our time telling us reality does not exist still gives us vision, beliefs, and opportunities. Imagine the answer to the question: "Do we receive information only through our known senses or are we each also hooked into a collective part of our being?"[2] Business applications would be revolutionary! So whether it is about quantum physics or another discipline, the questions are the drivers of discoveries and for business, in the end, they are the drivers of performance. The fascinating association here is that more than ever scientific questions are being answered with extraordinary findings and discoveries. It only makes sense that business, like science, conducts more experiments to enhance the value proposition. Scientific experiments have many of the elements and outputs that we seek to have when we conduct experiments in business: teams, problems, discoveries, assumptions, implications, findings, questions, solutions, and views. Go beyond the quantum and "create a company where everyone gives their best."[3] Make everyone understand the business model and participate in sustaining it as creating value is everyone's job.

The business model is the new center of gravity reflecting reality. This module expands it as a strategic collaborative tool by understanding and using all the components to manage the business model-centric organization.

Characteristics of a Sound Business Model Agenda

The purpose of an agenda is to achieve a goal, solve problems, and resolve issues. Using a business model agenda as an approach to collaborate can provide productive goal achievement, more solutions, and reduce the number of problems and issues. This collaborative approach helps transform companies and engages all levels of management and staff in continuous business model thinking to fulfill objectives and resolve issues before they become problems. If your employees are well aware of the company's business model as described in Module 1, they are in the best position to contribute ideas and spearhead experiments to keep it relevant, profitable, and sustainable. Business model collaboration happens across the entire organization and, as such, employees should be encouraged to (i) submit questions or ideas about their operational areas in the form of a story stating the perceived impact on the value proposition, resources, and capabilities; (ii) become part of an *ad-hoc* business model team with one member of management on each team to review submissions; (iii) engage in an experiment; (iv) make decision recommendations; (v) lead the implementation.

This module addresses how to collaborate to build a business model-centric organization. It consists of innovation teams made up of employees from all levels of the organization. For years, the focus has been on strategy. Now the business model drives strategy and constitutes the source of a successful strategy. Given the extensive discussions of business models in the popular press, collaboration around the business model is a necessary internal process feeding iteratively into the strategic plan, the financial plan, and the operational plan.

The Module Interrelationships: Setting the Collective Agenda for the Business Model-Centric Organization

Throughout the modules, you have been engaged in developing a boardroom agenda in each of the 18 "Enter the Boardroom Series" examples. In this module, we apply the contents of each module to a connected agenda for each strategic responsibility role (C suite): chief executive officer (CEO), chief financial officer (CFO), chief operating officer (COO). Each agenda connects into the strategic plan, the financial plan, and the operational plan to be used as living documents.

The purpose of an agenda is to set the priorities. In this context, the priorities to develop an adaptable and relevant business model-centric organization come from combining the key components of each module to determine what needs to be worked on to create more value with the business model. Together the agenda action items act as drivers of growth, performance, and value. (Below are a total of 20 priority areas.)

The Business Model Agenda (Module 1)

Given the interrelationships of the modules on the centric role of the business model, the agenda for Module 1 consists of only one absolute priority. (The other components of the business model are presented explicitly as priorities under the profit-making agenda and capabilities agenda and they are implicit in all the others.)

1. Clearly understand the value proposition, its implications, and impact.

The Profit-Making Agenda (Module 2)

Profits tell you whether the business model is working. The agenda for profitability focuses on the drivers of business model performance. There are three areas of financial priorities that determine the success of a business model. Each area requires specific action items to engage employees in contributing to the profit-making agenda.

1. Use revenue drivers to keep and expand revenue streams.
2. Relate cost drivers to resources and capabilities of the business model.
3. Adapt the value chain to your profit drivers.

The Strategic Direction Agenda (Module 3)

There are five areas of priorities when setting a strategic direction agenda from a business model perspective. Each area requires specific action items to engage employees in contributing to the strategic direction agenda.

1. Develop a vision that will activate your company's capacity to change.
2. Define your company's mission reflective of the value proposition.
3. Let your business model generate your strategies.
4. Set strategic and financial objectives that will ensure a relevant business model.
5. Make investment decisions in strategic assets to minimize costs, increase revenues, and deliver value.

The Capabilities Agenda (Module 4)

Capabilities are fundamental to business model performance. Developing the right capabilities requires a deep understanding of how they will allow your company to gain a competitive advantage. It is more than simply understanding your operations better. There are three areas of priorities to build capabilities to ensure a successful business model. Each area requires specific action items to engage employees in contributing to the capabilities agenda.

1. Identify the strategic resources needed to build dynamic processes.
2. Use dynamic processes to develop competencies that support a unique business model to result in a competitive advantage.
3. Add to your strategic resources with strategic alliance partners.

The Strategy Agenda (Module 5)

Strategies grow revenues if well executed. To execute a strategy well, you need a good business model. There are three areas of priorities to develop good strategies for a business model-centric organization. Each area requires specific action items to engage employees in contributing to the strategy agenda.

1. Allocate resources to execute the business model cost-driven and revenue-driven strategies.
2. Choose growth strategies such as integration or related diversification to build on the business model capacity for competitive advantage.
3. Challenge the assumptions and develop new strategies.

The Innovation Agenda (Module 6)

Innovation is the most critical capacity of an organization because it impacts the business model over time. There are five areas of priorities to create a capacity to innovate in a business model-centric organization. Each area requires specific action items to engage employees in contributing to the innovation agenda.

1. Create a culture of innovation wrapped around your business model.
2. Establish key drivers of innovation as the basis of your innovation strategy.
3. Define process and product innovation in terms of the business model.
4. Make innovation everyone's responsibility by creating innovation teams.
5. Use innovation teams to conduct innovation experiments.

New Incentives

Employees are at the core of a business model-centric organization. To create such an organization, each agenda should be governed by new incentives:

1. Divide up the work week to incentivize engagement.
2. Focus on across-the-organization work teams to incentivize innovation.
3. Give every agenda project a life by giving it a name to incentivize accomplishment.

Collaborate for Engagement

The underlying value of engaging all employees in the business model is that they are the agents of the business model. Their ability for unique problem solving is a matter of both innovation and change for an organization. Employees who look at innovation and change with a business model view create an organization that has a deep capacity for innovation and an ability to integrate changes with little if any resistance. Organizations have limits to change that are often visible by increased levels of employee resistance. The business model-centric organization can transform resistance into acceptance with employee engagement strategies for embracing new operational, financial, and strategic adaptations.

Opportunity Risk

Risk is a trade-off between opportunity and failure. A state of risk is a company's state of engagement. If a company does not engage employees by providing them with meaningful opportunities, it risks losing its business model impact. From a business model perspective, those opportunities are experiments embedded in the business model collaboration process. In the book *The Future of Management,* Gary Hamel speaks of related concepts such as enabling activism, experimentation beats planning, and distributed leadership.[4] One academic study points to the importance of business models that allow for creative managing (Appendix B).

Value Creation for a Business Model

Below is a framework inspired by the Porter value chain that brings together the key components of each module for a collective view of how a business model-centric organization creates value.

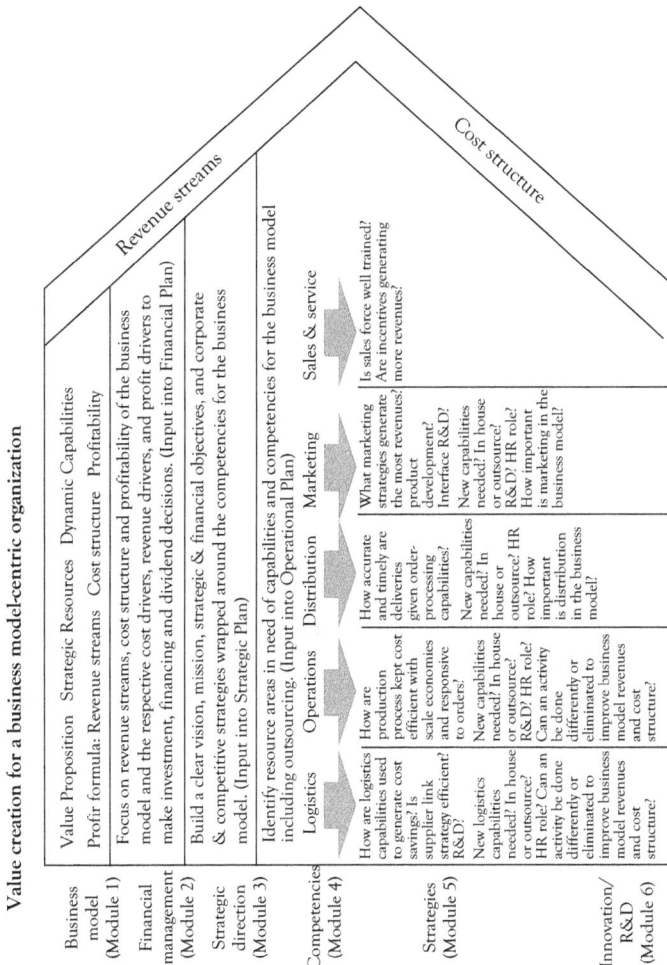

Value creation for a business model-centric organization

(Revenue streams — Cost structure)

	Logistics	Operations	Distribution	Marketing	Sales & service
Business model (Module 1)	Value Proposition Strategic Resources Dynamic Capabilities — Profit formula: Revenue streams Cost structure Profitability				
Financial management (Module 2)	Focus on revenue streams, cost structure and profitability of the business model and the respective cost drivers, revenue drivers, and profit drivers to make investment, financing and dividend decisions. (Input into Financial Plan)				
Strategic direction (Module 3)	Build a clear vision, mission, strategic & financial objectives, and corporate & competitive strategies wrapped around the competencies for the business model. (Input into Strategic Plan)				
Competencies (Module 4)	Identify resource areas in need of capabilities and competencies for the business model including outsourcing. (Input into Operational Plan)				
Strategies (Module 5)	How are logistics capabilities used to generate cost savings? Is supplier link strategy efficient? R&D?	How are production process kept cost efficient with scale economies and responsive to orders?	How accurate and timely are deliveries given order-processing capabilities?	What marketing strategies generate the most revenues? product development? Interface R&D?	Is sales force well trained? Are incentives generating more revenues?
Innovation/ R&D (Module 6)	New logistics capabilities needed? In house or outsource? HR role? Can an activity be done differently or eliminated to improve business model revenues and cost structure?	New capabilities needed? In house or outsource? R&D? HR role? Can an activity be done differently or eliminated to improve business model revenues and cost structure?	New capabilities needed? In house or outsource? HR role? How important is distribution in the business model?	New capabilities needed? In house or outsource? R&D? HR role? How important is marketing in the business model?	

Business Model Agenda Application

This is the last application in the "Enter the Boardroom" series. To learn the interrelationships among the six modules leading to the business model agenda, we focus on only one example to make the company a business model-centric organization.

Enter the Boardroom Interactive Applications

The "Enter the Boardroom" series have consisted of brief stories of companies to illustrate key concepts in each module. In this example, you are making a presentation to the board of Facebook to discuss priorities to become a business model-centric organization and to develop a strategic plan, a financial plan, and an operational plan. To be in an interactive learning environment, read the Facebook scenario below with the corresponding concept and reflect on who should be at the table, what the agenda should consist of, and what the outcome(s) might be.

Enter the Boardroom Series: Business Model Agenda

The Facebook Story

Facebook's initial public offering was originally valued at approximately $100 billion. Today the company's market capitalization is closed to $65 billion. There are several reasons for the fall in market value. Facebook's main source of revenue is advertising. The revenue growth is declining due to Facebook users' shift to smartphones where the company has far less paid ad formats. This mobile shift is also decreasing its payments business.[5] On the one hand, Facebook is confronting a great deal of concern about its business. On the other hand, some investors believe that with so many users and so much data about them, Facebook is "destined to be the most lucrative advertising platform in the world."[6] (For more information on the Facebook story, read the article cited in the notes and references starting on p. 157.)

This module shows that the strategic planning process must be interrelated, collaborative, and agenda driven. In this "Enter the

(*Continued*)

Boardroom" application you must develop a business model agenda for Facebook. Use the list of 20 priority areas to select the most critical areas for Facebook and generate action items under each priority. Use the agenda to prepare a strategic plan, operational plan, and financial plan that will make Facebook a business model-centric organization.

What is a Strategic Plan?

A strategic plan consists of a strategic vision, a business mission, objectives and priorities for action to improve performance. Companies engage in strategic planning to be relevant and competitive. A strategic plan for a business model-centric organization focuses on a clear vision, a current business mission, strategic and financial objectives, and strategies to achieve a competitive advantage with the business model.

What Is a Financial Plan?

A financial plan shows why the investments required for each priority will produce desired returns. It represents the financial outcomes of the strategic plan and operational plan. A financial plan for a business model-centric organization clearly demonstrates the revenue streams, cost structure, and profitability of the business model by identifying the cost drivers, revenue drivers, and profit drivers to inform the investment and financing decisions.

What Is an Operational Plan?

An operational plan is the result of the strategic priorities in the strategic plan. It represents action items to execute those strategic priorities. An operational plan for a business model-centric organization identifies resource areas in need of capabilities and competencies to support the business model.

(Continued)

Enter the Facebook Boardroom

You are one of the members of the board
Turn Facebook into a business model-centric organization

Guidance for the Manager:

Key Points on the Business Model Agenda

- A business model-centric organization needs a collective agenda.
- An agenda for a business model-centric organization is developed from the priorities of each module to strategically manage the organization.
- The strategic plan for a business model-centric organization focuses on a clear vision, a current business mission, strategic and financial objectives, and strategies to achieve a competitive advantage with the business model.
- The business model framework facilitates the strategic planning process to be interrelated, collaborative, and agenda driven.
- The business model drives strategy and engages employees from all levels to build a business model-centric organization.

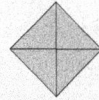

Add your own key points:

Below is a recommended Harvard Business Publishing case available for purchase at: www.hbsp.harvard.edu

ZARA: Fast Fashion

Pankaj Ghemawat; Jose Luis Nueno
Product Number: 703497-PDF-ENG
Revision Date: December 21, 2006
Publication Date: April 01, 2003
Length: 35 pages

Note: Description is from www.hbsp.harvard.edu with permission
"Focuses on Inditex, an apparel retailer from Spain, which has set up an extremely quick response system for its ZARA chain. Instead of predicting months before a season starts what women will want to wear, ZARA observes what's selling and what's not and continuously adjusts what it produces and merchandises on that basis. Powered by ZARA's success, Inditex has expanded into 39 countries, making it one of the most global retailers in the world. But in 2002, it faces important questions concerning its future growth."

Link to Module 7: This case is an excellent example of a business model-centric organization.

Below is a recommended Harvard Business Publishing articles available for purchase at: www.hbsp.harvard.edu

Reinvent Your Business Before It's Too Late

Paul Nunes; Tim Breene
Product Number: R1101D-PDF-ENG
Publication Date: January 01, 2011
Length: 9 pages

Description:

"To survive over the long haul, a company must reinvent itself periodically, jumping from the flattening end of one business performance curve to the rising slope of another. Very few companies make the leap successfully when the time comes. That's because they start the reinvention process too late. Once existing business begins to stall and revenue growth drops significantly, a company has less than a 10% chance of ever fully recovering. Accenture's Nunes and Breene, reporting on the results of their long-running High Performance Business research program, point to a striking difference between companies that have successfully reinvented themselves and those that failed. High performers manage their businesses not just along the growth curve of their revenues but also along three much shorter, though equally important, S curves: tracking the basis of competition in their industry, renewing their capabilities, and nurturing a ready supply of talent. By planting the seeds for new businesses before revenues from existing ones begin to stall, these companies enjoy sustained high performance."

Link to Module 7: This article suggests ways to recognize revenue and cost issues as causes to reexamine your business model.

How to Design a Winning Business Model

Ramon Casadesus-Masanell; Joan E. Ricart
Product Number: R1101G-PDF-ENG
Publication Date: January 01, 2011
Length: 9 pages

Description:

"Most executives believe that competing through business models is critical for success, but few have come to grips with how best to do so. One common mistake, the authors' studies show, is enterprises' unwavering focus on creating innovative models and evaluating their efficacy in standalone fashion-just as engineers test new technologies or products. However, the success or failure of a company's business model depends largely on how it interacts with those of the other players in the industry. (Almost any business model will perform brilliantly if a company is lucky enough to be the only one in a market.) Because companies build them without thinking about the competition, they routinely deploy doomed business models. Moreover, many companies ignore the dynamic elements of business models and fail to realize that they can design business models to generate winner-take-all effects similar to the network externalities that high-tech companies such as Microsoft, eBay, and Facebook often create. A good business model creates virtuous cycles that, over time, result in competitive advantage. Smart companies know how to strengthen their virtuous cycles, undermine those of rivals, and even use them to turn competitors' strengths into weaknesses."

Link to Module 7: This article keys on the dynamic elements of business models and the virtuous cycles for sustainable competitive advantage.

Below is a recommended Harvard Business Publishing exercise available for purchase at: www.hbsp.harvard.edu

BCPC Internet Strategy Team: An Exercise

Amy C. Edmondson; Laura R. Feldman
Product Number: 604035-PDF-ENG
Publication Date: October 03, 2003
Length: 4 pages

Description:

"This short fictional case forms the basis of a team decision-making exercise. The case, inspired by a real decision facing a major telecommunications company, describes a cross-functional management team convened by the CEO for the purpose of developing a recommendation about whether to conduct a full-scale launch of a new high-speed Internet access service. In the class session, groups of six participants are asked to conduct team meetings to arrive at a consensus about the launch decision—drawing from the information contained in the shared case and from privately held information contained in individual role sheets provided separately to each member. Although different team members hold very different perspectives about the launch, teams can arrive at thoughtful recommendations by working together to share their knowledge."

Link to Module 7: This team exercise is an innovative approach to make decisions with inputs from different areas within the organization.

Note: Descriptions are from www.hbsp.harvard.edu printed with permission.

Reflect on what you originally included on the first page of this module and how your understanding of the interrelationships of the modules has changed. Are you ready to transform your company to a business model-centric organization?

Appendices

A. Companies with Successful Business Models

Company	Value proposition	Capabilities	Revenue streams	Costs	Link
Netflix	Low-cost movie rentals and streaming	Massive selection, high quality streaming, accessibility on a variety of devices	Subscription based	Marketing, logistics, licensing	http://seekingalpha.com/article/304029-revamping-netflix-s-business-model
Pandora Media	Free access to online radio service	Customer options, accurate musical preferences based upon artist, title, or genre	Ad based	Royalties for music, general overhead	http://seekingalpha.com/article/363661-pandora-profitability-on-the-way-business-model-is-strong er-than-it-appears
Apple	Provide consumers with reliable and user-friendly technological products	Extremely appealing products to variety of consumer bases, user friendly, ground breaking technology	Product based and subscription based	R&D, marketing, customer support, technological support, manufacturing	http://businessmodelinstitute.com/apples-business-model-before-and-after-jobs-2-0/
Twitter	Allows anyone to interact socially with virtually anyone else	Ease of use, accessibility on a variety of devices, instantaneous information availability	Ad based	General overhead and maintenance	http://news.cnet.com/8301-1023_3-57323939-93/jack-dorsey-twitters-business-model-based-on-serendipity/
YouTube	Allows anyone to upload or view videos on whatever they desire	Free to use, unlimited potential, vast leader in video uploading and viewing	Ad based	General overhead and maintenance	http://seattletimes.nwsource.com/html/businesstechnology/2014490175_youtube14.html

Google	Provides consumers with search engine, maps, social networking, and more	World leader in search engine results, supreme quality of products and detail	Ad based	R&D, marketing, manufacturing, general overhead, and maintenance	http://www.npr.org/templates/story/story.php?storyId=13051841 2
Amica	Mutual company that excels in providing insurance in home, auto, marine, life, and other forms	Fantastic customer service, accessibility to clients	Client based	Marketing, benefits, insurance claims, general overhead	http://www.forbes.com/sites/robertreiss/2010/12/21/amicas-simple-secret-do-the-right-thing/
Budweiser	Provides premium drinks to consumer's variety of taste and alcoholic drink preferences	Historical foothold in industry, variety of products to adapt to preferences, generally low prices	Product based	Manufacturing, marketing, R&D, general overhead	http://articles.businessinsider.com/2010-02-11/strategy/30011687_1_innovation-global-director-products
NASCAR	Provides fans with exciting racing experience and provides sponsors access to fans' interests	Sponsorships, international media exposure	Ad based and contracts	Contracts, marketing, general overhead	http://www.speedwaymedia.com/?p=16774
Dunkin Donuts	Provides consumers with variety of food and beverage products in a timely manner	Store locations, quick service, variety of products, low cost to consumers	Product based	Resources, marketing, maintenance and upkeep, general overhead	http://www.businessweek.com/magazine/content/04_51/b3913090.htm

B. Academic Studies on Business Models

Research question	Data and methodology	Findings	Theory	Publication	Link	Module
Do scholars agree on what a business model is?	Innovation, business model, value creation, value capture, and strategy	Business model is a new unit of analysis, seeks to explain how value is created, and emphasizes system level approach	System Level Thinking	*The Journal of Management*	http://jom.sagepub.com/content/early/2011/04/29/0149206311406265	1
Do low-cost airlines assimilate their business models succesfully in mergers?	Mergers, business model, price discrimination, and yield management	Takeovers have a net beneficial effect as a consequence of introducing business models	Yield Management Pricing System	Law Borough University	http://www.lboro.ac.uk/departments/sbe/RePEc/lbo/lbowps/dobson_piga_mergers_LCA.pdf	2
Can we develop a business model that is driven by sustainability concepts?	Corporate sustainability, system sustainability, and sustainable business model	In order to develop a sustainable business model, an organization must develop internal structural and cultural capabilities	Neoclassical Economic Theory	Organization and Environment	http://www.cfsgs.com/uploads/3/6/0/1/3601225/103.pdf	3
How does technology partnerships allow business models to accomplish more?	Open innovation, businss models, co-development, and technology partnerships	R&D capabilities are core critical or contextual for the business model innovation	Co-development Relationships	Industrial Research Institute	http://cms.sem.tsinghua.edu.cn/semcms/res_base/semcms_com_www/upload/home/store/2008/7/3/2978.pdf	4

Are business models and product market strategies compliments or substitutes?	Product market strategy, business model, performance and competitive strategy	Business models and product market strategies go very well hand in hand as compliments	Contingency Theory	The Strategic Management Journal	http://www.slideshare.net/Alistercrowe/the-fit-between-product-market-strategy-and-business-model	5
How do we bridge the gap between encouraging creativity and the constraints of creativity?	Business model, business creativity, and constraints	There is a compromise between freedom and constraints, to keep idea generation going	Hevner Et Al's Design Science Research Framework	University of Lausanne	http://www.google.com/url?sa=t&rct=j&q=&esrc=s&source=web&cd=1&ved=0CE8QFjAA&url=http%3A%2F%2Fciteseerx.ist.psu.edu%2Fviewdoc%2Fdownload%3Fdoi%3D10.1.1.174.4711%26rep%3Drep1%26type%3Dpdf&ei=7WetT-OUPIKa8gTOgv2aDQ&usg=AFQjCNGE050Rz4t4Ev-GkZceeoPpqgaeVA	6
Are business models useful?	Business model and creative managing	Stating business models as models is rewarding to us because it allows us to see how they embody multiple and mediating rules	Model Theory	Long Range Planning Journal	http://www.cassknowledge.com/sites/default/files/article-attachments/517-~~business_models_as_models.pdf	7

C. *Image Credits*

Page number	Photo name	Company's boardroom	Image contributor	Web site
11	Teamwork with idea light bulbs	Netflix	Master isolated images	FreeDigitalPhotos.net
12	Conference hall and graph	Wal-Mart	Nokhoog_buchachon	FreeDigitalPhotos.net
14	Meeting room	eBay	Sixninepixels	FreeDigitalPhotos.net
35	3 D men in business meeting	Google	David Castillo Dominici	FreeDigitalPhotos.net
36	Business Meeting	Best Buy	Ddpavumba	FreeDigitalPhotos.net
37	3 D conference room	Tumblr	David Castillo Dominici	FreeDigitalPhotos.net
53	3 D persons on meeting	Yahoo!	David Castillo Dominici	FreeDigitalPhotos.net
54	Meeting hall	Nike	Nokhoog_buchachon	FreeDigitalPhotos.net
56	Meeting room	Nokia	Dan	FreeDigitalPhotos.net
69	The division of the world	Microsoft	Njaj	FreeDigitalPhotos.net
70	Meeting table and chairs at beach	Avon	David Castillo Dominici	FreeDigitalPhotos.net
72	Multinational meeting	Samsung	Ventrilock	FreeDigitalPhotos.net
88	Business meeting concept	Yum	David Castillo Dominici	FreeDigitalPhotos.net
90	Team meeting	Kellogg	Jscreationzs	FreeDigitalPhotos.net
92	Interior of modern office	Amazon	David Castillo Dominici	FreeDigitalPhotos.net
106	Business success	RIM	Ddpavumba	FreeDigitalPhotos.net
108	Business people around graph	Zynga	Suphakit73	FreeDigitalPhotos.net

Page number	Photo name	Company's boardroom	Image contributor	Web site
109	Watching the world	HP	Renjith Krishnan	FreeDigitalPhotos.net
128	Teamwork target	Facebook	Jscreationzs	FreeDigitalPhotos.net

Notes

Module 1

1. Starbird (2009).
2. Afuah and Tucci (2001).
3. Zott, Amit, and Massa (2011).
4. Magretta (2004).
5. Starbird (2009).
6. Helix Investment Management (2012).
7. Sloan (2011).
8. Helix Investment Management (2012).
9. Sloan (2011).
10. Helix Investment Management (2012); and Sloan (2011).
11. Swisher (2012).
12. Helix Investment Management (2012).
13. Sloan (2011).
14. Sechler (2012).
15. Sechler (2012).
16. Sechler (2012).
17. Sechler (2012).
18. Woo and Sherr (2012).
19. Talley and Banjo (2012).
20. Woo (2011).
21. Magretta (2004).

Module 2

1. Higgins (2007), p. xiii.
2. Efrati (2012), p. B6.
3. Efrati (2012), p. B6.
4. Vascellaro (2012), pp. A1–A6.
5. Letzing (2012), p. B6.
6. Solsman and Lamar (2012), p. B10.
7. Loten (2012), p. B6.

Module 3

1. Efrati (2012).
2. Swisher (2012).
3. Efrati (2012).
4. Efrati (2012).
5. Stubbs and Cocklin (2008), pp. 103–127 (see Appendix B).
6. Porter (1985).
7. Perlroth (2012).
8. http://investor.apple.com/faq.cfm?FaqSetID=6
9. Efrati (2012).
10. http://nikeinc.com/pages/about-nike-inc
11. http://www.nokia.com/global/about-nokia/company/about-us/about-us/
12. Clifford and Lattman (2012).

Module 4

1. Voltaire (1981).
2. Eisenhardt and Martin (2000).
3. Teece et al. (1997).
4. Thompson, Strickland, and Gamble (2005).
5. Barker (2012).
6. Lublin, Rockoff, and Glazer (2012).
7. Ramstad (2012).
8. Iyer and Davenport (2008).

Module 5

1. Maeda (2006).
2. Chasan and Murphy (2012), p. B5.
3. McKinsey and Company (2011).
4. Letzing and Efrati (2012), p. B4.
5. Jargon (2012).
6. Jakab (2012), p. C1.
7. Jargon and Chon (2012), pp. B1–B2.
8. Jargon and Chon (2012), pp. B1–B2.
9. Woo and Letzing (2012), pp. B1–B2.
10. Bensinger (2012), pp. B1–B4.
11. Glazer (2012).

Module 6

1. Richter (1980).
2. Richter (1980).
3. Anthony (2010).
4. Anthony (2010).
5. Sinfield, Calder, McConnell, and Colson (2011).
6. Christensen and Raynor (2003).
7. Martin (2011), pp. 82–87.
8. Korn (2011).
9. Jaruzelski and Holman (May 15).
10. Austen (2012), pp. B1–B5.
11. Jaruzelski and Holman (May 15).
12. Winkler (2012), p. B10.
13. Raice (2012), pp. B1–B2.
14. Letzing and FitzGerald (2012), p. B2.
15. Worthen and Tibken (2012), pp. B1–B2.
16. http://www.hpl.hp.com/open_innovation/
17. Bensinger (2012), pp. B1–B4.
18. Ovide and Letzing (2012).
19. Ovide and Letzing (2012).
20. Ovide (2012).

Module 7

1. Talbot (1986).
2. Talbot (1986).
3. Hamel and Breen (2007).
4. Hamel and Breen (2007).
5. Raice (2012).
6. Sengupta (2012).

References

Afuah, A., & Tucci, C. L. (2001). *Internet business models and strategies:* Text and cases. New York: Irwin/McGraw-Hill.

Anthony, S. (2010). *Four innovation lessons from Anheuser-Busch.* Retrieved May 10, 2012, from Harvard Business Review Web site: http://blogs.hbr.org/anthony.2010/02/four_innovation_lessons_from_a.html

Austen, I. (2012, June 29). In setback, RIM delays blackberry's next version. *The New York Times*, pp. B1–B5.

Barker, T. (2012, April 10). Microsoft goes online shopping at AOL. *The Wall Street Journal*, p. C10.

Bensinger, G. (2012, July 27). Amazon's margins evaporate. *The Wall Street Journal*, pp. B1–B4.

Chasan, E., & Murphy, M. (2012, June 5). The big number. *The Wall Street Journal*, p. B5.

Christensen, C. M., & Raynor, M. E. (2003). *The innovator's solution: creating and sustaining successful growth.* Cambridge, MA: Harvard Business School Press.

Clifford, S., & Lattman, P. (April 6, 2012). *Pressed from all Sides, Toys 'R' Us fights to reinvent itself.* Retrieved May 1, 2012, from The New York Times Online Web site: http://www.nytimes.com/2012/04/07/business/toys-r-us-last-of-the-big-toy-stores-tries-to-reinvent-itself.html?pagewanted=all

Efrati, A. (2012, January 20). Google cools off, and stocks drops. *The Wall Street Journal*, p. B6.

Efrati, A. (2012, January 20). New display ad push adds to bag of tricks. *The Wall Street Journal*, pp. B6.

Efrati, A. (2012, June 25). *At Yahoo, last year's plan is tossed.* Retrieved July 1, 2012 from The Wall Street Journal Online Web site: http://online.wsj.com/article/SB10001424052702304441404577478691454611910.html

Efrati, A. (2012, July 17). Google's Mayer takes over as Yahoo Chief. *The Wall Street Journal*, pp. B1–B2.

Efrati, A., & Vascellaro, J. E. (2012, July 18). Yahoo's profit lags. *The Wall Street Journal*, p. B7.

Eisenhardt, K. M., & Martin, J. A. (2000). Dynamic capabilities: what are they? *Strategic Management Journal 21*(10/11), 1105–1122.

Glazer, E. (2012, April 12). A David and Gillette story. *The Wall Street Journal*, p. B1.

Hamel, G., & Breen, B. (2007). *The future of management*. Boston, MA: Harvard Business School Press.

Helix Investment Management (2012). *Pandora: Profitability on the way, business model is stronger than it appears*. Retrieved August 1, 2012, from Seeking Alpha Web site: http://seekingalpha.com/article/363661-pandora-profitability-on-the-way-business-model-is-stronger-than-it-appears

Higgins, R. C. (2007). *Analysis for financial management* (8th ed.). New York: McGraw-Hill Irwin.

Iyer, B., & Davenport, T. H. (2008, April). Reverse engineering Google's innovation machine. *Harvard Business Review*, pp. 58–68.

Jakab, S. (2012, April 18). Winning recipe at Yum won't last forever. *The Wall Street Journal*, p. C1.

Jargon, J. (2012, February 21). Boss talk: Yum's CEO serves up new taco, growth plans. *The Wall Street Journal*, p. B7.

Jargon, J., & Chon, G. (2012, February 16). A hunch for crunch: Kellogg adds snacks. *The Wall Street Journal*, pp. B1–B2.

Jaruzelski, B., & Holman, R. (2011). *The three paths to open innovation*. Retrieved May 15, 2012, from Strategy-Business Web site: www.strategy-business.com

Korn, M. (2011). *Top innovators rank low in R&D spending*. Retrieved February10, 2012, from The Wall Street Journal Online Web site: http://online.wsj.com/article/SB10001424052970203752604576645401657833270.html

Letzing, J. (2012, May 17). Google rolls out smarter search. *The Wall Street Journal*, p. B6.

Letzing, J., & Efrati, A. (2012, June 28). Google's new role as gadget maker. *The Wall Street Journal*, p. B4.

Letzing, J., & FitzGerald, D. (2012, July 27). At Zynga, business game is tough. *The Wall Street Journal*, p. B2.

Loten, A. (2012, May 17). Can Tumblr turn a profit? *The Wall Street Journal*, p. B6.

Lublin, J. S., Rockoff, J. D., & Glazer, E. (2012, April 10). Avon picks a CEO from J&J. *The Wall Street Journal*, p. B1.

Maeda, J. (2006). *The laws of simplicity*. Cambridge, MA: The MIT Press.

Magretta, J. (2004, May). Why business models matter. *Harvard Business Review*.

Martin, R. L. (2011, June). The innovation catalysts. *Harvard Business Review*, pp. 82–87.

McKinsey & Company (2011, January). *Creating more value with corporate strategy: McKinsey global survey results*. Retrieved November 1, 2011, from McKinsey Quarterly Web site: http://www.mckinseyquarterly.com/Creating_more_value_with_corporate_strategy_McKinsey_Global_Survey_results_2733

Ovide, S (2012, August 13). Groupon staff feel the heat. *The Wall Street Journal*, p. B1.

Ovide, S., & Letzing, J. (2012, August 14). *Groupon's shares hit new lows after results*. Retrieved August 16, 2012, from The Wall Street Journal Online Web site: http://online.wsj.com/article/SB10000872396390444184704577588943041800350.html

Perlroth, N. (2012, July 17). Mayer hopes to brighten user experience at Yahoo. *The New York Times*, pp. B1–B4.

Porter, M. (1985). *Competitive advantage*. Boston, MA: Harvard Business School Press.

Raice, S. (2012, July 27). Facebook's growth slows. *The Wall Street Journal*, pp. A1–A2.

Raice, S. (2012, August 6). Zynga's rocky shift to mobile. *The Wall Street Journal*, pp. B1–B2.

Ramstad, E. (2012, April 9). Samsung's profit hits fast track. *The Wall Street Journal*, p. B6.

Richter, I. (Ed.) (1980). *The notebooks of Leonardo da Vinci*. Oxford, UK: Oxford University Press.

Sechler, B. (2012, June 20). FedEx CEO predicts industry shift. *The Wall Street Journal*, p. B9.

Sengupta, S. (2012, August 13). A steep climb back. *The New York Times*, pp. B1–B5.

Sinfield, J. V., Calder, E., McConnell, B., & Colson, S. (2011, December 21). How to identify new business models. *MIT Sloan Management Review, Winter 2012, 53*(2).

Sloan, P. (2011). *Jack Dorsey: Twitter's business model based on 'serendipity'*. Retrieved April 5, 2012, from News - CNET Web site: http://news.cnet.com/8301-1023_3-57323939-93/jack-dorsey-twitters-business-model-based-on-serendipity/

Solsman, J. E., & Lamar, M. (2012, May 23). Best Buy's profit drops 25%. *The Wall Street Journal*, p. B10.

Starbird, M. (2009). *Mathematics from the visual world*. Chantilly, VA: The Great Courses.

Stubbs, W., & Cocklin, C. (2008). Conceptualizing a "sustainability business model". *Organization and Environment, 21*, pp. 103–127.

Swisher, K. (2012, March 6). Yahoo to reshape operations. *The Wall Street Journal*, p. B7.

Talbot, M. (1986). *Beyond the quantum*. New York: Macmillan Publishing Company.

Talley, K., & Banjo, S. (2012, May). With more on its shelves, Wal-Mart results rise. *The Wall Street Journal*, p. B1.

Thompson, A. A., Strickland, A. J., & Gamble, J. (2005). *Crafting and executing strategy: The quest for competitive advantage, concepts and cases* (14th ed.). New York: McGraw-Hill/Irwin.

Vascellaro, J. E., (2012, March 20). Apple pads investor wallets. *The Wall Street Journal,* pp. A1–A6.

Winkler, R. (2012, July 20). Handsets on a RIM and a prayer. *The Wall Street Journal,* p. B10.

Woo, S. (2011, February 11). EBay revs up PayPal engine. *The Wall Street Journal,* p. B1.

Woo, S., & Letzing, J. (2012, February 1). Amazon's spending habit hurts profit. *The Wall Street Journal,* pp. B1–B2.

Woo, S., & Sherr, I. (2012, January 26). Netflix recovers subscribers. *The Wall Street Journal,* pp. B1–B4.

Worthen, B., & Tibken, S. (2012, August 9). H-P to book $8 billion charge. *The Wall Street Journal,* pp. B1–B2.

Zott, C., Amit, R., & Massa, L. (2011, July). The business model: Recent developments and future research. *Journal of Management, 37*(4), pp. 1019–1042.

Index

OTHER TITLES IN OUR STRATEGIC MANAGEMENT COLLECTION

William Q. Judge, Collection Editor

- *Building Strategy and Performance Through Time: The Critical Path* by Kim Warren
- *A Leader's Guide to Knowledge Management: Drawing on the Past to Enhance Future Performance* by John Girard
- *An Executive's Primer on the Strategy of Social Networks* by Mason Carpenter
- *Fundamentals of Global Strategy: A Business Model* by Cornelis de Kluyver
- *Operational Leadership* by Andrew Spanyi
- *Dynamic Strategies for Small Businesses* by Sviatoslav Steve Seteroff
- *Strategic Analysis and Choice: A Structured Approach* by Alfred Warner
- *Building Organizational Capacity for Change: The Leader's New Mandate* by William Q. Judge
- *Designing the Networked Organization* by Ken Everett
- *Managing for Ethical-Organizational Integrity: Principles and Processes for Promoting Good, Right, and Virtuous Conduct* by Abe Zakhem and Daniel Palmer
- *Moral Leadership: A Transformative Model for Tomorrow's Leaders* by Cam Caldwell
- *Knowledge Management: The Death of Wisdom: Why Our Companies Have Lost It— and How They Can Get It Back* by Arnold Kransdorff

---

Announcing the Business Expert Press Digital Library

Concise E-books Business Students Need for Classroom and Research

This book can also be purchased in an e-book collection by your library as

- a one-time purchase,
- that is owned forever,
- allows for simultaneous readers,
- has no restrictions on printing, and
- can be downloaded as PDFs from within the library community.

Our digital library collections are a great solution to beat the rising cost of textbooks. e-books can be loaded into their course management systems or onto student's e-book readers.

The **Business Expert Press** digital libraries are very affordable, with no obligation to buy in future years. For more information, please visit **www.businessexpertpress.com/librarians**. To set up a trial in the United States, please contact **Adam Chesler** at *adam.chesler@businessexpertpress .com* for all other regions, contact **Nicole Lee** at *nicole.lee@igroupnet.com*.